UNBREAKABLE

DEFYING GRAVITY WITH THE WORD OF GOD

Shannon Cromwell Brown

M.ED. REHABILITATION COUNSELING

Copyright 2017 by Shannon Brown

All rights reserved. Printed in the United States of America. No parts of this book may be used or reproduced in any manner whatsoever without written permission except in the case of brief quotations embodied in critical articles for review.

Unless otherwise noted, scripture quotations are taken form the Holy Bible: King James Version (KJV), New International Version (NIV), and the Message Version (MSG). All scriptures have been referenced according.

Shannon Brown titles may be purchased in bulk for educational training purposes. For information you may email: authorshannonbrown@gmail.com.

Library of Congress Cataloging- in Publication Data

UNBREAKABLE: Defying Gravity with the Word of God/ Shannon Brown

ISBN: 978-0-692-99736-9

DEDICATION

This book is dedicated to my three precious blessings, my children- Samuel Christopher, Alexia Thomasina and Antonio Austin. You are my heartbeat. You give me unconditional love and the courage to face each day. I love you all so very much. During the most difficult days of my life, just looking into your faces gives me encouragement and determination to go on and not to give up. I am so very proud of each of you. Your personalities, individual gifts and talents make you extraordinary. You babies have blessed my life. I am a better individual because of you and I thank God, each day for allowing me to be your mother. You are truly my three little miracles. I love you... And to my little angle in heaven, my sweet baby boy, William Floyd, thank you for teaching your mama her very first true lesson in faith and trusting God. I love you and you will forever be in my heart....

Foreword

Scripture abounds with verses that clearly descend one's nature to give. Therefore, as we are created in His image, our nature should also be to give. However, if we mistakenly believe God to be a taker, we will subconsciously begin to conform to this distorted image of God, thereby causing us to become takers. When you want something you've never had, you must do something you've never done. Equipped with this powerful knowledge, you will be in a position to fulfill your scriptural duty as a child of the King of Kings and the Lord of Lords. This is the spirit of God that lives inside of my beloved daughter, Shannon C. Brown. The spirit of life; the spirit of tenacity; the spirit of defying the odds; the spirit of pressing beyond the limits; the spirit of love; the spirit of hope and the warm spirit of giving. This is where the true heart of this book lies, which mirrors the very image of Shannon's soul. She is simply giving to others what God has given to her.

Furthermore, through powerful scriptures and through Shannon's eloquent words of expression, UNBREAKABLE will forever change your life and is sure to strengthen your faith in the All Mighty God.

Shannon Cromwell Brown

This is one of the proudest moments a father, who is also a pastor can have; to have his child choose to serve God by sharing the word and encouraging world to be free and at peace in Jesus Christ our Lord. May your lives be deeply enriched by Unbreakable…Defying Gravity with the Word of God by my lovely daughter, Shannon Cromwell Brown.

"I can do all thing through Christ who strengthens me" Philippians 4:13. Pressing beyond your limits

Nathaniel Robinson, Sr, Pastor (Father of the Author)

Eastside Missionary Baptist Church

584 Meeting Street

Downtown Charleston, SC

Acknowledgement

I would like to acknowledge my mother Delores Knight and my deceased grandparents, Samuel and Thomasina Cromwell for raising me with the values of character and integrity. Thank you for teaching me the power of love and compassion while equipping me with a strong foundation in Christ. You've taught me to always believe in myself and to never follow the crowd; to be different, to be "me." Thank you for teaching me how to be a Godly mother to my children and raise them up in the Lord. Thank you to my father and stepmother, Reverend & Mrs. Nathaniel & Jestine Robison, Sr for your love and guidance throughout the years. I would also like to thank all my siblings, family and friends for all your love, support and encouragement.

A special thank you to Rena Monk (model), Monica Benson Wilson (hair stylist/ fashion stylist), Idalan Haymon (makeup artist), Jaz Clos, Sidney Conley (photographer-model images) and Gary Davis of Sterling Photography (cover & back images).

Introduction

In life we are faced with so many challenges each day. Most of them we face before we even walk out of our own front door. We step out into the world daily and do our best to manage our personal business and private affair so strategically, that no one would ever imagine what we are in fact dealing with. We put on our game faces, dressed to the nine and head to the office, school, church, the grocery store, our private businesses, the gym and so on, looking as normal as possible, as we attempt to fit in with the crowd of other seemingly normal individuals. As emotional beings, we tend to have the nature of hiding or concealing our problems as a protective mechanism to help us cope or deal with the issue. We simply refuse to allow outsiders the privilege of having a glimpse into our private matters. I myself, being guilty of this behavior as well. It is so common that at some point in our lives, if we are truly honest, we are all undeniably guilty.

In dealing with crises, many of us may reach out to family members, friends, co-workers or even strangers to help guide us through the chaos of our lives. But is this always the best thing? When it comes to your personal issues, you must always treat it with care and use caution. What may be right for one may not be good for another. Furthermore, sometimes it's best to keep others out of your business to avoid having your situation exposed by someone you felt was trustworthy enough to disclose such personal information to. However, there is only one resource that will never steer you wrong, and this is the word of God. As a child of God, it is the soul foundation that will keep you grounded and provide that solid direction and guidance that you need.

Unfortunately, everyone is not on the same level of spiritual maturity. When you are dealing with a gut-wrenching crisis and you are paralyzed with fear, it may be difficult to pick up the bible and find the individualized word that is needed immediately to provide comfort. A death, a devastating diagnosis, a troubled child, imprisonment, marital infidelity, physical abuse, financial devastation, betrayal etc… are just the tip of the iceberg of what we as individuals face each day and walk around as if all is well and when given the first opportunity of seclusion break down, curl up in a fetal position and cry out violently to God for help. In cases like these and many others, we need immediate access to a specialized word or scripture that is suitable for our situation and will provide us with comfort.

There are people in so much pain all over the world dealing with some heavy situations. This book is for those individuals; those who are in a battle; those who are fighting spiritually; those who need a strong word in a mighty way; those who are fragile and at the edge of breaking; the confused, the frightened, the lonely, the depressed, the brokenhearted. This is a book of hope, spiritual encouragement and inspiration to confirm that no matter what your circumstance is that you are going through, with the Lord God as your foundation, you can make it through. Yes, you may stumble and fall. You may even get bumped and bruised but rest assured, you will not break. The word gives us the strength and the courage to fight. It motivates us not to give up and helps us to become UNBREAKABLE!

Maximizing this book to the fullest

To maximize and get the most out of this book, you must first make sure you have your weapon, the Holy Bible, which is the absolute foundation of the book. (Note: this book brings translations from the New King James, King James, New International and the Message Versions of the Holy Bible). Whatever version you choose, make sure it is in a translation that you are comfortable with and can comprehend with ease.

Next, you must decide the best time for meditation. I strongly recommend meditating first thing in the morning before any outside influences can settle in and disrupt your spirit. Do not begin to prep for the day: such as picking out wardrobe or putting breakfast on. Nothing! The only thing I see that may help you to become more alert is getting a cup of coffee, but nothing else; and please do not turn on the radio. Again, this will interrupt and disturb the flow of your spirit and mind which can prevent you from meditating.

Thirdly, you must find a designated place to meditate and study. Find a place of peace, a place with very limited distractions. Set your atmosphere to receive the spirit of the Lord. Pray, meditate through song or worship music or whatever it is to prepare you heart and mind to receive and welcome the spirt. Have special songs of meditations. Although hearing the word of God through song is inspirational, not all gospel or worship songs are for you and some may not minister to your spirit in the way you desire, hence you should be selective in your music and make it applicable to your situation, your battle, your fight.

Finally, have some writing material handy to record your thoughts and revelations, as the spirit reveals them to you. This will help in your daily meditation and review. It will also help to measure your growth in the months to come. I wish you success in your journey of healing and restoration. This will be one of the best investments you will ever make. Enjoy…

TABLE OF CONTENTS

Chapter 1: Unbreakable -Unmasking Your True Self 13

Chapter 2: 26Unbreakable - One Flesh, The Marriage 26

Chapter 3: Unbreakable – The Body – The Temple 40

Chapter 4: Unbreakable – My Children, My Fruit 48

Chapter 5: Unbreakable - Enemies 56

Chapter 6: Unbreakable - Heartache 63

Chapter 7: Unbreakable – Kin Folk - Family 69

Chapter 8: Unbreakable – Forever Thankful 78

Chapter 9: Unbreakable – Betryal or Loyalty 85

Chapter 10: Unbreakable – The Lost 90

Chapter 11: Unbreakable – Self Control 109

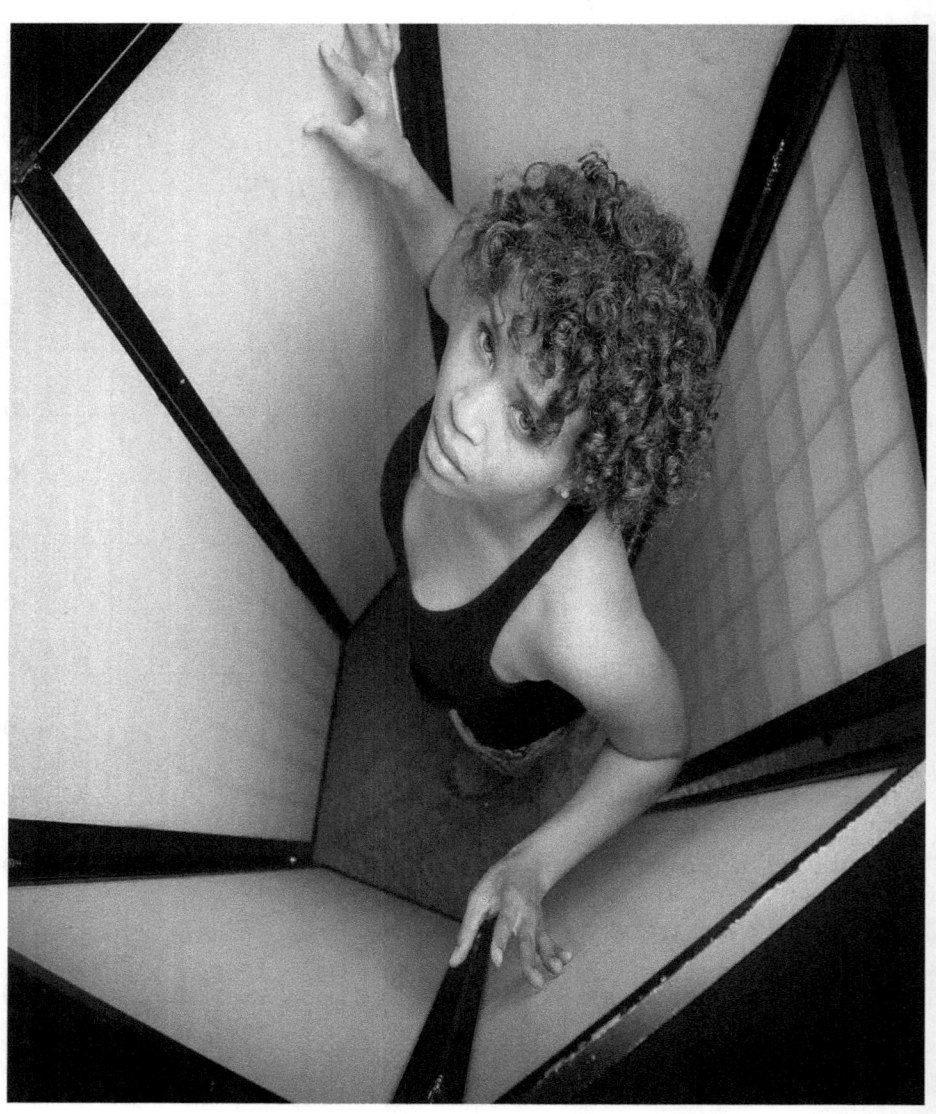

CHAPTER 1

UNBREAKABLE- Unmasking Your True Self

Who are you? This seems like a very simple question, doesn't it? It doesn't seem to be too complex; after all, it is only made up of three small words, carrying three letters each. Funny, what appears to be a basic question, "who are you?", most people find it very difficult to answer. Some even spend their entire lifetime searching for the answer while wearing a mask every single day.

Some of us are masked with the lies and untruths told to us by others. We tend to identify ourselves through the lenses of others. Many have been told such things as: "You will never be anything", "You can't do that" "You are so ugly", "You are stupid", "You are just like..." etc.... Unfortunately, we allow this poison to saturate our minds and toxify our total inner soul.

One very important point I would like to express is... "DO NOT SEE YOURSELF THROUGH ANOTHER PERSON'S LENSES!" You must logically and realistically analyze this person's credibility or lack thereof. At what level of integrity do they operate? It is absolutely, preposterous to receive what others think of you and take it as the gospel truth. I need you to ask yourself a question. "Who are these people and what gives them the authority to cast such judgement on me?" Their view of you depends upon so many distorted variables. Where are they spiritually, emotionally, physically, financially, academically, professionally? What is their level of character?

Furthermore, analyze the dynamics of the relationship. Is this someone who verbally attacks you in an aggressive way or constantly belittles you? If so, this individual is very damaging to your overall well-being. It is strongly advised that you re-evaluate this relationship and possibly end it for the sake of your peace of mind, mental health and most importantly, your safety. On the contrary, if the above actions describe your behavior towards other individuals (which goes against the character and integrity of God) yes, you may very well receive backlash and judgement from it. However, you need to repent and sincerely ask God for forgiveness, as well as to the individuals you have offended. Don't be an obstruction to your own peace and blessings. Operate with Godly character and integrity and make the situation right. Some individuals may even need counseling, anger management classes, etc.... whatever it takes, do it. Do it for yourself!

Furthermore, in unmasking our true self we must know what our virtues are. What do you stand for? What and who will you sacrifice for? What will you not surrender to? What values do you wake up with daily? What legacy do you want to leave behind for your children, your family, your community? Today, re-evaluate your life, your behaviors. Are you operating according to your virtues? Take off your mask and recommit to the man or woman of God that you desire to be deep in your heart, mind and soul. The person you see in the mirror that others don't know.

The motto that I live by is a quote by William Shakespeare: "Know thyself and to Thine own self be true." If something doesn't give you peace in your spirit, how can you continue? You may for a period, but eventually the rubber will meet the road and you will have to make an important decision. In knowing myself, personally, I know that I am a Christian and I use the word of God as my compass to give me guidance each day. By no means am I perfect, but I do know that I am a child of God and I am a work in progress.

Moreover, if you believe that God sent his Son Jesus to die for our sins that we may have abundant life, you too are a Christian. You must know without a doubt, that you are indeed His child no matter what others think or say about you. Operate with the character of God and walk in alignment to His word and truth. God has outlined who we are in his word and we must never depart from it. Keep this word close to your heart and meditate on it day and night. We are beautiful beings made in his image.

As we unmask our true selves and tear down the walls of doubt, lies and confusion, look to God for our "true" identity. It is more prudent to view ourselves through God's eyes, for He is the one that truly loves us unconditionally. He loved us first before we even knew Him. This is what is true: the opinions of others are irrelevant. Have joy and peace in knowing that God loves you just the way you are, a beautifully sculpted masterpiece created in his loving image.

Scriptures for Unmasking your True Self:

So, you are no longer a slave, but God's child; and since you are his child, God has made you also an heir. **Galatians 4:7 NIV**

And you are complete in Him, who is the head of all principality and power. **Colossians 2:10 NIV**

For God so loved the world that he gave his one and only Son, that whoever believes in him shall not perish but have eternal life. **John 3:16 NIV**

I can do all things through Christ who gives me strength **Philippians 4:13 NIV**

If you fully obey the Lord your God and carefully follow all his commands I give you today, the Lord your God will set you high above all the nations on earth. **Deuteronomy 28:1 NKJV**

You are of God, little children, and have overcome them, because He who is in you is greater than he who is in the world. **1 John 4:4 NKJV**

Do not lie to one another, since you have put off the old man with his deeds, and have put on the new man who is renewed in knowledge according to the image of Him who created him. **Colossians 3:9-10 NKJV**

"Blessed shall you be in the city, and blessed shall you be in the country. **Deuteronomy 28:3 NKJV**

In righteousness you shall be established; You shall be far from oppression, for you shall not fear; And from terror for it shall not come near you. **Isaiah 54:14 NKJV**

"Blessed shall be your basket and your kneading bowl. **Deuteronomy 28:5 NKJV**

Give, and it will be given to you: good measure, pressed down, shaken together, and running over will be put into your bosom. For with the same measure that you use, it will be measured back to you. **Luke 6:28 NKJV**

The Lord shall cause your enemies who rise up against you to be defeated before your face: they shall come out against you one way, and flee before you seven ways. **Deuteronomy 28:7 NKJV**

And the peace of God, which surpasses all understanding, will guard your hearts and minds through Christ Jesus. **Philippians 4:7 NKJV**

"The Lord shall command the blessing on you in your storehouses and in all to which you set your hand, and He will bless you in the land which the Lord your God is giving you. **Deuteronomy 28:8 NKJV**

The Lord will establish you as a holy people to himself, just as He has sworn to you, if you keep the commandments of the Lord your God, and walk in His ways. **Deuteronomy 28:9 NKJV**

Then all people of the earth shall see that you are called by the name of the Lord, and they shall be afraid of you. **Deuteronomy 28:10 NKJV**

And the Lord will grant you plenty of goods, in the fruit of your body, in the increase of your livestock, and in the produce of your ground, in the land of which the Lord swore to give you. **Deuteronomy 28:11 NKJV**

The Lord will open to you His good treasure, the heavens, to give the rain to your land in its season, and to bless all the work of your hand. You shall lend to many nations, but you shall not borrow. **Deuteronomy 28:12 NKJV**

And the Lord will make you the head and not the tail; you shall be above only, and not be beneath, if you heed the commandments of the Lord your God, which I command you today, and are careful to observe them. **Deuteronomy 28:13 NKJV**

And my God shall supply all your needs according to His riches in glory by Christ Jesus. **Philippians 4:19 NKJV**

"Blessed shall be the fruit of your body, the produce of your ground and the increase of your herds, the increase of your cattle and the offspring of your flocks. **Deuteronomy 28:4 NKJV**

She gets up while it is still night; she provides food for her family… **Proverb 31:18 NIV**

She speaks with wisdom, and faithful instruction is on her tongue. **Proverb 31:26 NIV**

She is clothed with strength and dignity… **Proverbs 31:25**

For it is by grace you have been saved, through faith- and this is not from yourselves, it is the gift of God **Ephesians 2:8 NIV**

But thanks be to God! He gives us the victory through our Lord Jesus Christ. 1 **Corinthians 15:57 NIV**

Blessed shalt thou be when thou comest in, and blessed shalt thou be when thou goest out. **Deuteronomy 28:6**

This is how we know who the children of God are and who the children of the devil are: Anyone who does not do what is right is not God's child, nor is anyone who does not love their brother and sister. **1 John 3:10 NIV**

And whoever does not carry their cross and follow me cannot be my disciple **Luke 14:27**

Then Jesus said to his disciples, "Whoever wants to be my disciple must deny themselves and take up their cross and follow me. **Matthew 16:24 NIV**

Rooted and built up in him, strengthened in the faith as you were taught, and overflowing with thankfulness. **Colossians 2:7 NIV**

With God we will gain the victory, and he will trample down our enemies. **Psalm 108:13 NIV**

If you declare with your mouth, "Jesus is Lord," and believe in your heart that God raised him from the dead, you will be saved. **Romans 10:9 NIV**

Nay, in all these things we are more than conquerors through him that loved us. **Romans 8:37 KJV**

3Surely he shall deliver thee from the snare of the fowler, and from the noisome pestilence. 4He shall cover thee with his feathers, and under his wings shalt thou trust: his truth shall be thy shield and buckler. **Psalms 91:3-4 KJV**

Affirmations for Unmasking your True Self:

- ❖ I am a Child of God. I am an heir of the King and have the favor of God. I prosper in all aspects of my life.
- ❖ I am a child of God and I obey his commandments. I am blessed wherever my feet trod. I am blessed in every location, environment, situation and circumstance. I am blessed on every street, of every city, of every state, of every country, and of every continent of this earth. I AM BLESSED!
- ❖ I have everlasting life. God sent his son Jesus to die for my sins therefore, no matter what evil forces come up against me, I am the victor. I fight, and I win every time with Jesus.
- ❖ I am a believer in Christ. I do not perish but have abundant life despite the evil actions of my enemies. God died and rose for my sins and I am saved by his blood.
- ❖ I am a new creature in Christ Jesus. My mind and spirit have been renewed. I think differently and behave differently. I am no longer the same person. The old person is dead. I now operate in the knowledge and in the image of Christ who is my creator.

- ❖ I am a protected child of God. I cannot be touched. The Lord allows my enemies to rise up against me, only to be destroyed right before my very eyes. They all run and scatter in fear for my Lord is mighty in power.
- ❖ I walk according to the word of God and his teachings. He blesses the works of my hands and causes them to create riches. I have an abundance of blessings. I do not borrow but in fact, have an overflow to lend to others in need.
- ❖ I have the peace of God which surpasses all understanding and circumstance. My heart and mind are clear, and I am not worried about anything or anyone in Jesus' name.
- ❖ My womb is blessed (the womb of my wife is blessed) because I am a blessed and obedient child of the King. I do what is pleasing in His sight and He gives me the desires of my heart.
- ❖ Yet while the enemy attempts to break my spirit with slander, hate and evil works, I remain strong in the Lord and walk with dignity and Godly character.
- ❖ God blesses my business and everything my hand touches. He blesses my land and allows it to produce abundantly because He is pleased with my obedience.
- ❖ The more I am cast down and attacked by man, the higher God raises me up. He makes me stronger and wiser. He equips me with tools to manifest victory; for God is my shield and my buckler.

- ❖ I am a faithful child of the King who obeys His laws. For my obedience, He blesses all my comings and goings. I am forever covered.
- ❖ I am focused. I accomplish all my daily duties and responsibilities with great success while yet, I nurture and care for my family. God has given me the spirit of excellence and I can do all things through Christ Jesus who strengthens me.
- ❖ I have no lack in my life. My family and I have food, clothing, shelter, transportation, financial security, excellent health, love, peace and joy. My God supplies all my needs according to his abundant riches in glory through Christ Jesus.
- ❖ I am covered by the blood and have a sound mind in Christ. He equips me with the ability to speak wisdom and to use proficient judgement.
- ❖ I am a child of God, I have the resounding strength to do all things with God's help.
- ❖ I am valuable. I take time to invest in myself through education, training, physical fitness, wellness and healthy life choices to allow personal growth, development and the expansion of my territory. I am precious in the sight of God and He has a preeminent plan for my life.
- ❖ I have an undeniable standard for my life and how I deserve to be treated by others.
- ❖ I have God almighty living within me and greater is the God that lives in me, than the evil that lives in this world. I have no fear.

- ❖ I am a remarkable child of God with great value. I focus and uphold the Godly standards that Christ has set for my life. I am not manipulated by people nor by my emotions. I stand on the word of God because it is truth and shall never change.
- ❖ I am formed and made in the righteousness of Jesus Christ. Oppression and worry are far away from me. I do not fear anyone or any situation because terror does not come near me.
- ❖ I know who I am in Christ Jesus. I need not prove myself to anyone. God has established my foundation and I am confident in this. I have the confidence of Christ and walk in His authority.
- ❖ God is the supreme creator; therefore, I see myself through the eyes of God and not of others. I am perfectly and wonderfully created in His image.
- ❖ I am a blessed child of the King and carry the presence of God daily. People take note and fear to come up against me because they see the mighty power of Jesus on my life.
- ❖ I stand firm in the face of adversity. I do not run nor; do I bow down. I take challenges head on, with the boldness and the confidence of God. I am more than a conqueror.
- ❖ I am a covered child of the king. God delivers and protects me from all evil forces which lie, mock and wish me ill will. They are dumbfounded and confused that I am unharmed; for God is my secret place and He hides me safely under his wings.
- ❖ I am a giver and I do it out of love, compassion and of a cheerful heart. In return, out of my abundant giving I receive

Unbreakable

blessings of good measures, pressed down, shaken together and running over.

CHAPTER 2

UNBREAKABLE- One Flesh, The Marriage

Marriage is a beautiful institution. It is a holy covenant between a man, a woman and God. At times things may be in sync and well balanced. Everything is good and harmonious. However, other times devastating storms may brew that can rock the marriage foundation to the very core. Issues can range within a wide spectrum with harsh realities such as infidelity, poor communication or financial hardship to which can impact the stability of a marriage in various degrees. Consequently, because marriage is built on the word of God, He must always be the center of it. As a God believing christian, the most powerful way to conquer any marital situation is to apply the word and your faith to it, in order to fight against all principalities that may create a threat to your marriage.

Furthermore, before a husband and wife can fight as one body in Christ, they both must receive the word of God as truth; as LAW. It shall be the absolute final say! There shall be no inclusion or exclusion nor picking or choosing of the word to serve a selfish purpose. The word of God is sharper than a two-edged sword and it will cut you. **"For the word of God is alive and active. Sharper than any doubled-edged sword, it penetrates even to dividing soul and spirit, joints and marrow, it judges the thoughts and attitudes of the heart." Hebrews 4:12 NIV.** The word can make us feel good about our actions but it can also make us feel bad about our actions. It convicts us but doesn't condemns us. It is this very thing, the conviction of the word, that helps us to remain on the path of righteousness or helps us to return to the path of righteousness.

We all have sinned, but through the blood of Jesus Christ which was shed on the cross and accepting him as your Lord and Savior, they are all washed away. The beauty of the word is that if you receive it humbly with a childlike heart, the right attitude and a Godly spirit, it can indeed, shape, mold and strengthen your marriage. The word provides the marriage with the Godly armor it needs to fight against the weapons of the enemy that attempts to destroy your sacred union as husband and wife.

Scriptures for Marriage:

Therefore, shall a man leave his father and his mother, and shall cleave unto his wife: and they shall be one flesh. **Genesis 2:24 KJV**

"Haven't you read", he replied, "that at the beginning the Creator made them male and female, and said, for this reason a man will leave his father and mother and be united to his wife **Matthew 19:4 NIV**

"Wherefore they are no more twain, but one flesh. What therefore God hath joined together, let not man put asunder." **Matthew 19:6 KJV**

"Wives, understand and support your husbands in ways that show your support for Christ. The husband provides leadership to his wife the way Christ does to his church, not by domineering but by cherishing. So just as the church submits to Christ as he exercises such leadership, wives should likewise submit to their husbands." **Ephesians 5:22-24 MSG**

Husbands, go all out in your love for your wives, exactly as Christ did for the church- a love marked by giving, not getting. Christ's love makes the church whole. His words evoke her beauty. Everything he does and says is designed to bring the best out of her, dressing her in dazzling white silk, radiant with holiness. And that is how husbands out to love their wives. They're really dong themselves a favor- since they're already "one" in marriage. **Ephesians 5:25-28. MSG**

So, ought men to love their wives as their own bodies. He that loveth his wife loveth himself. **Ephesians 5:28 KJV**

Nevertheless, let every one of you in particular so love his wife even as himself and the wife see that she reverences her husband. **Ephesians 5:33 KJV**

A wife of noble character who can find? **Proverb 31:10 NIV**

She is worth far more than rubies. Her husband has full confidence in her and lacks nothing of value. **Proverb 31:11 NIV**

She brings him good, not harm all the days of her life. **Proverb 31:12 NIV**

Whoso findeth a wife findeth a good thing, and obtaineth favour of the Lord. **Proverbs 18:22 KJV**

Let the deacons be the husbands of one wife, ruling their children and their own houses well. **1 Timothy 3:12 KJV**

Nevertheless, to avoid fornication, let every man have his own wife, and let every woman have her own husband. **1 Corinthians 7:2 KJV**

House and riches are the inheritance of father: and a prudent wife is from the Lord. **Proverbs19:14 KJV**

Husbands, love your wives, and be not bitter against them. **Colossians 3:19 KJV**

Then Joseph being raised from sleep did as the angel of the Lord had bidden him, and took unto him his wife: **Matthew 1:24 KJV**

Let the husband render unto the wife due benevolence: and likewise, also the wife unto the husband. **1 Corinthians 7:3 KJV**

The wife hath not power of her own body, but the husband; and likewise, also the husband hath not power of his own body, but the wife. **1 Corinthians 7:4 KJV**

Her Husband is known in the gates, when he sitteth among the elders of the land. **Proverbs 31:23 KJV**

Her children arise up, and called her blessed; her husband also, and he praiseth her. **Proverbs 31:28 KJV**

Jesus saith unto her, Go, call thy husband, and come hither. **John 4:15 KJV**

Wives, submit yourselves unto your own husbands, as it is fit in the Lord. **Colossians 3:18 KJV**

A virtuous woman is a crown to her husband; but she that maketh ashamed is as rottenness in his bones. **Proverbs 12:4 KJV**

The heart of her husband doth safely trust in her, so that he shall have no need of spoil. **Proverbs 31:11 KJV**

That they may teach the young women to be sober, to love their husbands, to love their children, **Titus 2:4 KJV**

If any be blameless, the husband of one wife, having faithful children not accused of riot or unruly. **Titus 1:6 KJV**

Scriptures of Forgiveness in Marriage

But if you do not forgive others their sins, your Father will not forgive your sins. **Matthew 6:15 NIV**

And forgive our debts, as we forgive our debtors. **Matthew 6:12 NIV**

Look upon mine affliction and my pain; and forgive all my sins. **Psalms 25:18 NIV**

For thou, Lord, art good, and ready to forgive; and plenteous in mercy unto all them that call upon thee. **Psalms 86:5 NIV**

Take heed to yourselves; If thy brother trespass against thee, rebuke him; and if he repents, forgive him. **Luke 17:3 NIV**

And forgive us our sins; for we also forgive every one that is indebted to us. And lead us not into temptation; but deliver us from evil. **Luke 11:4 NIV**

31Get rid of all bitterness, rage and anger, brawling and slander, along with every form of malice. 32Be kind and compassionate to one another, forgiving each other, just as in Christ God forgave you. **Ephesians 4:31-32**

If we confess our sins, he is faithful and just to forgive us our sins, and to cleanse us from all unrighteousness. **1 John 1:9 NIV**

Then came Peter to him, and said, Lord, how oft shall my brother sin against me, and I forgive him? Till seven times? Jesus saith unto him," I say not unto thee Until seven times: but Until seventy time seven." **Matthew 18:21-22 KJV**

The fruit of that righteousness will be peace; its effect will be quietness and confidence forever. **Isaiah 32:17 NIV**

Let us not become weary in doing good, for at the proper time we will reap a harvest if we do not give up. **Galatians 6:9 NIV**

<u>Scriptures for Separation in Marriage</u>:

But and if she departs, let her remain unmarried, or be reconciled to her husband; and let not the husband put away his wife. **1 Corinthians 7:11 NIV**

And the woman which hath a husband that believeth not, and if he be pleased to dwell with her, let her not leave him. **1 Corinthians 7:13 KJV**

For the unbelieving husband is sanctified by the wife, and the unbelieving wife is sanctified by the husband; otherwise your children would be unclean, but now they are holy. **1 Corinthians 7:14 NKJV**

For the rest of you who are in mixed marriages- Christian married to non-Christian- we have no explicit command from the Master. So, this is what you must do. If you are a man with a wife who is not a believer but who still wants to live with you, hold on to her. If you are a woman with a husband who is not a believer but he wants to live with you, hold on to him. The unbelieving husband shares to an extent in the holiness of his wife, and the unbelieving wife is likewise touched by the holiness of her husband. Otherwise, your children would be left out; as it is, they also are included in the spiritual purposes of God. **1Corinthians 7:12-14 MSG**

On the other hand, if the unbelieving spouse walks out, you've got to let him or her go. You don't have to hold on desperately. God has called us to make the best of it, as peacefully as we can. You never know, wife: The way you handle this might bring your husband not only back to you but to God. You never know, husband: The way you handle this might bring your wife not only back to you but to God. **1Corinthians 7:15-16 MSG**

And don't be wishing you were someplace else or with someone else. Where you are right now is God's place for you. Live and obey and love and believe right there. God, not your marital status, defines your life… **1Corinthians 7:17 MSG**

Scriptures for love in Marriage:

4 Love is patient, love is kind. It does not envy, it does not boast, it is not proud. **5** It does not dishonor others, it is not self-seeking. It is not easily angered, it keeps no record of wrongs. **6** Love does not delight in evil but rejoices with the truth. **7** It always protects, always trust, always hopes always preservers. **8** Love never fails… **1 Corinthians 13:4-8 NIV**

Husband Affirmations:

- ❖ Father, I trust you and your word. I have left the covering of my mother and father to join in holy covenant with (wife)_____ and because of this, we are no longer two, but one flesh in Christ.
- ❖ *Our marriage is a holy and sacred union covered by your blood of Christ. Therefore, I shall not let anything, anyone or any circumstance come between our marriage. Nothing will separate or break my bond with (wife)_____. Lord, I thank you for your eternal covering and protection over our marriage. Amen
- ❖ *I affirm that I am the head of my home. I will love and cherish (wife) _____. I will honor her by leading with Godly wisdom and example.
- ❖ I will not selfishly dominate (wife)_____ but will respect her, cover her, protect her and most

importantly, love her as Christ have loved the church. I will be held accountable by God for any actions that do not align with his word.

- ❖ I love (wife)_____ as I love my own body because we are one flesh. When I love her, care for her and protect her; I love, care and protect my very own body.
- ❖ I would never purposely inflict pain nor injury upon my very own body; and because (wife)_____ and I are the same flesh, I would never purposely inflict pain nor injury on her. In loving my wife, I love myself in return.
- ❖ (Wife)_____ has a strong Godly character. I am blessed to have her as my wife. She is good for me and enhances my life daily. Her value is priceless to me and our family.
- ❖ I am thankful and blessed to have (wife)_____ as my wife because according to the word of God she is a good thing; and by having her by my side, I have the favor of God on my life.
- ❖ I am the head of my home. I rule, guide and direct my wife, _____, and our children. I take complete responsibility over them as it has been designed by God. I cover my entire household with excellence in the name of Jesus.
- ❖ _____(wife) is a leader to other women. She leads by example through the Godly love and care she gives to me and our children before others.

- ❖ I have full confidence and satisfaction in(wife) _____. I lack nothing because she provides all that I need and desire.

- ❖ I love my wife, _____. I avoid all bitterness towards her but show her compassion, love, kindness and respect.

- ❖ When I am wrong and disobedient to God concerning (wife)_____, I repent to God. I put my selfish pride aside and humbly ask my wife for forgiveness. I am a man of character and take accountability for my actions.

- ❖ As the head of the house, I take responsibility to do all things necessary, according to the word, to get my home back in order. It is my responsibility to restore trust and security within my marriage and home. If I need to seek outside help to rebuild our marriage, I will because I love (wife)_____ as Christ loves the church and will do anything for her.

- ❖ I restore trust by consistently allowing my words to align with my actions. I hide no damaging secrets from (wife)_____ because I value our marriage; and I refuse to jeopardize it or destroy my family.

- ❖ Secrets will have absolutely no place in my marriage because it separates me from God and ultimately separates from (wife)_____. What God has joined together, let no one separate because my wife and I are one body in Christ.

- ❖ After God, (wife)_____ is my number one priority. It is my duty to always make her feel safe, secured, valued, loved and respected.
- ❖ I refuse to lie or withhold vital information from my (wife)_____. I will operate with integrity and respect our sacred covenant.
- ❖ Because I am the head of the household, I set the tone for my entire family. As I lead with Godly example, (wife)_____ and our family are secure, safe and at peace. When they are at peace, I am at peace.
- ❖ As a firm believer in Christ Jesus, I remain still and I cover _____ (wife) even if she does not believe in the word. The spirit of God that is within me has the power to touch her spirit and make her whole.

Wife Affirmations:

- ❖ I trust you, God and your word. I have left the covering of my mother and father to join in holy covenant with (husband)_____; and because of this, we are no longer two, but one flesh in Christ.
- ❖ Our marriage is a holy and sacred union covered by your blood. Therefore, I shall not let anything, anyone or any circumstance come between our marriage. Nothing will separate or break my bond with (husband)_____. Lord, I thank you for your eternal covering and protection over our marriage. Amen

- ❖ Because (husband) _____ is the head of our household, I submit to him. I allow him to lead and guide our family and I support him in doing so. This gives my husband the confidence to lead as a man, but most importantly, a man of God for our family.

- ❖ When I submit and trust (husband)_____ as the head of the home, I activate my faith in God; knowing that God will cover him and give him the wisdom and the knowledge as a Godly leader.

- ❖ I will trust (husband)_____ because he is a man of God who loves me as Christ loves the church. And because of this, I walk in faith that he will not misuse his authority regarding this Godly assignment nor, for the well-being of our marriage and family.

- ❖ I vow to always respect (husband)_____. If I am wrong or disobedient in my role as wife in any way, I repent and ask God for forgiveness. I humbly lay my pride aside and ask my husband for forgiveness.

- ❖ I restore trust to (husband)_____ by being consistent in my words and actions. I am an open book, withholding nothing from him. Secrets have no place in my marriage because secrets pull me away from God and create separation within my marriage.

- ❖ After God, (husband)_____ is my very first priority. It is my duty to love and respect him as head of the home. I will take care of his needs first above all others.

- ❖ I am the righteousness God. I am equipped to handle and manage all issues of our household concerning my husband, _____, and our family.
- ❖ _____(husband) is a respected man of God and he sits in the company of Godly men of valor and spiritual elders.
- ❖ I love (husband)_____. I avoid all bitterness towards him but, show him compassion, love, kindness and respect.
- ❖ (Husband)_____ has complete confidence in me. I am an asset to his life. My value is immeasurable because I am a Godly source of encouragement, comfort and support to my husband.
- ❖ As a godly wife, it is my responsibility to cover (husband)_____ daily as he goes into the world to provide and protect our family.
- ❖ As a firm believer in Christ Jesus, I remain still, and I cover _____ (husband) even if he is an unbeliever. The spirit of God that is within me has the power to touch his spirit and make him whole.

CHAPTER 3

UNBREAKABLE – The Body-The Temple

Our body is a jewel, comprised of many precious stones, strategically put together by God. God made us in his very own image and did so with the perfection, for He is a perfect God. He created us with different ethnicities; rich with multicultural facial features, beautiful shades of browns, creams, yellows and reds and in diverse shapes and sizes. Although we may have differences, we are yet affected by the same things in life, especially when it comes to sickness.

How do you handle sickness in your body? What is your spiritual mindset when physical challenges knock you or your family to its knees and leave you bewildered? Although we are ultimately responsible for the care and maintenance of our bodies, we sometimes come under attack. Sometimes no matter what we do, we can still experience serious issues with our health such as Cancer or Lupus. It is not uncommon to go into a state of panic or shock. Having something so heavy thrusted at you without warning, can become overwhelming and scary.

However, no matter what the situation is that we are facing, we must never forget the power of God. If it is His will for our lives, He will heal us completely. If He has another plan, where our situation is used as a teaching tool to impact the lives of others, He will teach. If our illness is used to bring families together, He will reunite. If the sickness is there to impact the world on a greater level; to demonstrate love and kindness and to bring Him glory, then He will use it.

God has His very own agenda and plan for our lives. He knew our journey before we were even born. But through it all, our roots must remain grounded in Christ Jesus, our true foundation. Jesus has the miraculous power to heal. He is God! He can turn destitute situations around even when they look hopeless. We must always keep our faith. No matter what it looks like, trust God, stand strong, be courageous and know, that our God is a mighty healer, indeed.

Scriptures for Healing:

And Jesus went about all Galilee, teaching in their synagogues, and preaching the gospel of the kingdom, and healing all manner of sickness and all manner of disease among the people. **Matthew 4:23 KJV**

How God anointed Jesus of Nazareth with the Holy Ghost and with power: who went about doing good, and healing all that were oppressed of the devil; for God was with him. **Acts 10:38 NIV**

And he said unto him, Arise, go thy way: thy faith hath made thee whole. **Luke 17:19 KJV**

He sent his word, and healed them, and delivered them from their destructions **Psalms 107:20 KJV**

Beloved, I wish above all thing that thou mayest prosper and be in health, even as thy soul prospereth. **3 John 1:2 KJV**

He heals the brokenhearted, and binds up their wounds. **Psalms 147:3 NIV**

And the prayer offered in faith will make the sick person well; the Lord will raise them up. If they have sinned, they will be forgiven. **James 5:15 NIV**

Heal me, Lord, and I will be healed; save me and I will be saved, for you are the one I praise. **Jeremiah 17:14 NIV**

For assuredly, I say to you, whoever says to this mountain, "Be removed and be cast into the sea," and does not doubt in his heart, but believes that those things he says will be done, he will have whatever he says. **Mark 11:23 NKJV**

Therefore, I say to you, whatever things you ask when you pray, believe that you receive them, and you will have them. **Mark 11:24 NKJV**

Who Himself bore our sins in His own body on the tree, that we, having died to sin, might live for righteousness- by whose stripes you were healed. **1 Peter2:24 NKJV**

Therefore, put on the full armor of God, so that when the day of evil comes, you may be able to stand your ground, and after you have done everything, to stand. **Ephesians 6:13 NIV**

Who forgiveth all thine iniquities; who healeth all thy diseases **Psalms 103:3 KJV**

But Jesus turned him about, and when he saw her, he said, Daughter, be of good comfort; thy faith hath made thee whole. And the woman was made whole from that hour. **Matthew 9:22 KJV**

31 And immediately Jesus stretch out his hand, and caught him, and said unto him, "O you of little faith, why did you doubt? 32 And when they got into the boat, the wind ceased. **Matthew 14:31 NKJV**

And Jesus, immediately knowing in Himself that power had gone out of Him, turned around in the crowd and said, "who touched My clothes"? **Mark 5:30 KJV**

And the Lord said, "If you have faith as a mustard seed, you can say to this mulberry tree, "Be pulled up by the roots and be planted in the sea" and it would obey you. **Luke 17:6 KJV**

But he was wounded for our transgressions, he was bruised for our iniquities; the chastisement of our peace was upon him and with his stripes we are healed. **Isaiah 53:5 KJV**

And when he had called unto him his twelve disciples, he gave them power against unclean spirits, to cast them out, and to heal all manner of sickness and all manner of disease. **Matthew 10:1 KJV**

And great multitudes followed him; and he healed them there. **Matthew 19:2 KJV**

Unbreakable

A merry heart doeth good like a medicine: but a broken spirit drieth the bones **Proverbs 17:22 KJV**

No weapon that is formed against thee shall proper; **Isaiah 54:17 KJV**

Jesus said unto him, "If you can believe, all things are possible to him who believes. **Mark 9:23 KJV**

And the whole multitude sought to touched him; for there went virtue out of him, and healed them all. **Luke 6:16 KJV**

But my God shall supply all your need according to his riches in glory by Christ Jesus. **Philippians 4:19 KJV**

Peace I leave with you, My peace I give to you: not as the world gives do I give to you. Let not your heart be troubled, neither let it be afraid. **John 14:27 NKJV**

For we walk by faith, not by sight: **2 Corinthians 5:7 KJV**

And Jesus saith unto him, I will come and heal him. **Matthew 8:7 KJV**

And the blind and the lame came to him in the temple; and he healed them. **Matthew 21:14 KJV**

And beholding the man which was healed standing with them, they could say nothing against it. **Acts 4:14 KJV**

Now faith is the substance of things hoped for, the evidence of things not seen. **Hebrew 11:1 KJV**

Affirmations for Healing:

- The healing power Jesus used to heal the crowds then, is the same healing power He uses today to heal my body. The Lord has all power in his hands and can heal all manner of sicknesses and diseases. I declare today that I am healed in Jesus' name.
- I have strong faith in Christ and He has the power to perform a complete healing miracle within my body. All things are possible through Christ Jesus and today I receive completed healing and wholeness in my body.
- No sicknesses or diseases will overtake my body. I am strong and healthy. I fight off all parasites, infections and viruses. No weapon that tries to attack my body will prosper. All foreign bodies will disappear and die. God protects me. He fights for me. I am covered the mighty blood of Jesus and I am healed.
- My God is almighty. His word heals my body and delivers me from destruction daily. I am strong and full energy. I live an active life. Each day my quality of life gets better and better in Jesus' name.
- I prosper in my health just as I prosper in my soul because God desires complete wholeness in my life. I am physically active, eat healthy and live a fruitful life full of joy and laughter.
- When I am hurt, brokenhearted or low in spirit, God covers me and binds up my wounds. He cares for me with love and compassion. He heals my entire body and restores joy to my spirit.

- ❖ I pray for my brothers and sisters in faith and believe in my heart that God will heal them. And because of my strong faith in Christ, the Lord makes them well and raises them up. They are strong, full of life and completely healed in the name of Jesus.

- ❖ I am confident in my Lord and savior and have radical faith in His power. I command sickness and disease to be removed from my body and I believe in my heart that I will have what I say.

- ❖ I am healed by the stripes of Jesus. I am free of sickness and disease. My body functions with perfection. My heart beats with timely precision. My blood pumps freely through my veins. Oxygen flows through my blood to each organ. My bones are strong and dense, and my mind is sharp. I am in perfect health in the name of Jesus.

- ❖ Cancer, Lupus, Diabetes, Hypertension, heart problems, Sarcoidosis, Arthritis, bone diseases, obesity, kidney failure, migraines, neurological damage, mental illness, ADHD and all manner of sickness and disease has no room in my body. I am whole and in perfect form. My arms and legs are strong. My back is strong! Each organ is strong and functions as God created it to function. Satan has no authority over my body for Jesus resides within. I am healed in Jesus' name. Amen!

CHAPTER 4

UNBREAKABLE- MY Children, My Fruit

Children are blessings from God. God has given us a designated assignment concerning our children. It is us, the parents, who He has made responsible for their lives. We are the most influential beings (other than God) that they will ever encounter within their lifetime. It is a big job and a huge responsibility and should never be made light of. We nurture them; feed them; clothe them; protect them; support them; enrich them; cultivate them; cover them; pray for them and most important, we love them unconditionally.

Furthermore, in showing love to our children, we make it a priority to teach them the ways of the Lord. This is the most profound act that a parent can ever do for his children. When we teach our children the word of God, we are teaching them to fight, but not in the physical realm- the spiritual. We are teaching them to be warriors of faith in this world filled with trying circumstances. Today the world is such a different place than how it used to be when you were a child. The remarkable advancement of technology has allowed the devil to enter your own home and attack your children without you even knowing it. They can be stalked, bullied and preyed upon right from their very bedroom while you may be sitting, obliviously, just 10 feet away.

Moreover, our children can be attacked by evil the very moment they step out the front door. This is not to scare you, rather this is the reality. This is evident in the daily news. Situations happen so fast for instance, your child can wake up in the morning, eat breakfast and kiss you goodbye and by the afternoon you can receive a phone call that your child was just in a car accident. Or perhaps they may leave to head for a party with friends in the twilight hours and the next thing you know you are getting a call from jail. Even more devastating, having your child drive 100 feet down to a gas station and get shot or fatally wounded in a carjacking. It happens all the time across the entire country. As a parent we must constantly cover our children in prayer with the word of God.

Granted, as parents it is inevitable that our children will grow up and become young adults and we must allow them that independence to grow and mature. However, teens still long for those boundaries to some degree, that we as parents set. This gives them a sense of security. They feel safe and protected. As they mature into young adults, we will have to allow them to spread their wings and stand on the foundation that we have instilled within them from their early childhood. But whether they are still in the home, off attending a college or university or they may even have a family of their own… a parent who is grounded in Christ will always make sure that their children are prayed for and covered by the word of God no matter the age or level. There is peace in knowing that God is in control and our children rest securely in His hands; and that all the teaching and the training that we have instilled in them through the years will resurface and they will be equipped to fight any battle that comes their way.

Scriptures for your Children:

Come, my children, listen to me: I will teach you the fear of the Lord. **Psalm 34:11 NIIV**

Children's children are a crown to the aged, and parents are the pride of their children. **Proverbs 17:6 NIV**

All your children will be taught by the Lord, and great will be their peace. **Isaiah 54:13 NIV**

Tell it to your children, and let your children tell it to their children, and their children to the next generation. **Joel 1:3**

Discipline your children, for in that there is hope: do not be a willing part to their death. **Proverb 19:18 NIV**

Dear children, keep yourselves from idols. **1 John 5:21NIV**

And, ye fathers, provoke not your children to wrath: but bring them up in the nurture and admonition of the Lord. **Ephesians 6:4 KJV**

A good person leaves an inheritance for their children, but a sinner's wealth is stored up for the righteous. **Proverbs 13:22 NIV**

Endure hardship as discipline; God is treating you as his children. For what children are not disciplined by their father? **Hebrews 12:7**

"First let the children eat all they want," he told her, "for it is not right to take the children's bread and toss it to the dogs". **Mark 7:27**

Children are a heritage from the Lord, offspring a reward from him. **Psalm 127:3 NIV**

Children, obey your parents in the Lord, for this is right. **Ephesians 6:1 NIV**

Fathers, provoke not your children to anger, lest they be discouraged. **Colossians 3:21 KJV**

A fool spurns a parent's discipline, but whoever heeds correction shows prudence. **Proverbs 15:5 NIV**

Whoever loves discipline loves knowledge but whoever hates correction is stupid. **Proverb 12:1 NIV**

Whoever disregards discipline comes to poverty and shame, but whoever heeds correction is honored **Proverbs 13:18 NIV**

Train up a child the way he should go: and when he is old, he will not depart from it. **Proverbs 22:6 KJV**

Affirmations Covering Children:

- ❖ My children are my blessing. They are forever my crown and treasures from God. My children are not burdens or heavy weights in my life but, my daily joy and sunshine. I thank God, every day for giving me these beautiful, precious miracles.
- ❖ I am the pride of my children. They hold me in high esteem and give me unconditional love. I am completely responsible for

what I teach my children through my word and actions. I am their first teacher and I hold the greatest influence of men on this earth. Therefore, I teach them the character of God through my behavior according to the word.

- ❖ I am a legacy for my children. I instill strong Godly values and morals within them that will be handed down to their children and their children's children.
- ❖ My children are taught of the Lord and will put no other God above Him. Their extracurricular activities nor their material possessions will take priority over him. God is first in the lives of my children.
- ❖ I work hard daily, gain knowledge and understand so that I can to leave an inheritance for my children.
- ❖ God is my father and the father of my children. They are not exempted from His discipline and the ruling of His mighty iron hand. It is for their ultimate growth and development as children of God.
- ❖ My children will never grow hungry. They will always be completely nourished and have an abundance of food for God is my sustainer.
- ❖ I teach my children to fear the Lord and respect his mighty power and authority through not only my words but through my actions.
- ❖ My children are a heritage from God. I value them as priceless jewels. They are my precious gifts from God.

- ❖ As I impress the word of God in the hearts and mind of my children, their lives are filled with peace, joy and clarity.

- ❖ My children obey the rules and the laws of my household even when they are compelled not to, because they fear and respect the Lord. They have the wisdom of God to know that as a parent, God gave me the authority to care, nurture, protect and correct them daily. They fall in line with my authority because it is right, according to the word of God.

- ❖ I motivate and encourage my children. I do not provoke them to anger. I strive to bring out the best in them by showing love and support. They come to me when they need Godly wisdom, guidance and direction. They trust me and feel safe and secure because I walk a life that shows undeniable faith in Christ.

- ❖ When my children go to school, they are covered by the blood of Jesus. They will not be bullied, harassed or intimidated. They fear no one. They walk in the authority of God and no weapon formed against them shall prosper.

- ❖ I provide Godly discipline and correction to my children for the in betterment of their lives. They are taught respect and obedience in the home so when they are out in the world, they know how to how to respect authority figures and walk with the character of God at all times.

- ❖ I nurture and direct my children with love and the wisdom of God. I am a loving parent but I am firm and direct. My children respect me because I walk with the authority of God in my home and teach them the ways of God.

- My children are covered by the blood and receive my Godly correction on their lives. I stand on the word of God always and teach them what is right. They are not tempted by the evil tricks of the devil. My children have a sound mind and apply the word of God in every situation.

- *My children avoid negative people, situations and environments which may create temptation. My children have the wisdom of God to make sound decisions every day. God has a divine purpose for their lives and they are destine for greatness.

- My children seek Godly wisdom and knowledge. They study and meditate on the word daily to develop a deeper relationship with the God. My children believe in the word and apply it to their lives. They are Godly examples to their peers.

- My children are guided by the Lord and take heed to Godly correction. I claim victory and a life full of prosperity over my children.

- I train my children in the ways of the Lord. They are grounded in His doctrines. When they come of age and it is time to leave the security of my home, they will always remember the ways of Lord. even when they older and leave home.

CHAPTER 5

UNBREAKABLE- Enemies

Blindly we walk through life, not knowing who we will encounter. Often, we are unaware of the motives or agendas of others when we first meet them. Some people are genuine, kind hearted beings, while others may be just the opposite. However, as children of God, our desire is to walk in Godly character by showing love and being kind to others without judgement. But how do we protect ourselves from those who wish not to do the same towards us?

Consequently, God helps us in this area of our lives but some of us tend to overlook the signs that He presents. God gives us the spirit of discernment when dealing with the enemy. When you feel that something just isn't right about an individual, listen to your inner gut. God is talking to you. How many times have you felt a certain type of energy about someone you meet? You couldn't put your finger on it but, felt in your spirit a sense of uneasiness; later to find that you were dead on. Take heed to these feelings and always proceed with caution when dealing with these types of individuals. They may in fact, have motives to harm you or bring discord and confusion to your life and that of your family.

However, enemies can also be those we have come to know and love. Unfortunately, those who we call friends and family can fall in this unsuspected category. As you probably would expect, this kind of enemy creates the deepest and most hurtful pain. The enemy comes to steal, kill and destroy. They may have desires to break up your marriage; to sabotage your job, hurt your children, destroy your business, create conflict within your family, etc.... We must watch out for those who attempt to do evil against us. God is angered by evil and has a way to deal with the wicked and those who choose to attack his children. However, no matter how hard they try, they will never be able to come up against the mighty wrath of God. Always remember to keep your faith, be still and know that He is God.

Scriptures for the Enemy:

No weapon that is formed against thee shall prosper; and every tongue that shall rise against thee in judgment thou shalt condemn. This is the heritage of the servants of the Lord, and their righteousness is of me, saith the Lord. **Isaiah 54:17 KJV**

Do not take revenge, my dear friends, but leave room for God's wrath, for it is written: "It is mine to avenge; I will repay" says the Lord. **Romans 12:19 NIV**

"The wrath of God is being revealed from heaven against all the godlessness and wickedness of people, who suppress the truth by their wickedness." **Romans 1:18 NIV**

God is a righteous judge, a God who displays his wrath every day. **Psalms 7:11 NIV**

Be alert and of sober mind. Your enemy the devil prowls around like a roaring lion looking for someone to devour. **1 Peter 5:8 NIV**

The wicked will see it and be grieved; He will gnash his teeth and melt away; The desire of the wicked shall perish. Psalms **112:10 NKJV**

There is no peace, "says the Lord, "for the wicked Isaiah **48:22 NKJV**

For the one in authority is God's servant for your good. But if you do wrong, be afraid, for rulers do not bear the sword for no reason. They are God's servants, agents of wrath to bring punishment on wrongdoers. **Romans 13:4 NIV**

Pour out your wrath on them; let your fierce anger overtake them. **Palms 69:24 NIV**

Let their own eyes see their destruction; let them drink the cup of the wrath of the Almighty. **Job 21:30 NIV**

He unleashed against them his hot anger, his wrath indignation and hostility- a band of destroying angels. **Psalm 78:49 NIV**

The desire of the righteous ends only in good, but the hope of the wicked only in wrath. **Proverbs 11:23 NIV**

For the arms of the wicked shall be broken, but the Lord upholds the righteous. **Psalms 37:17 NKJV**

The Lord lifts up the humble; He casts the wicked down to the ground Psalms **147:6 NKJV**

The Lord is at your right hand; he will crush kings on the day of his wrath. **Psalms 110:5 NIV**

See, the storm of the Lord will burst out in wrath, a driving wind swirling down on the heads of the wicked. **Jeremiah 23:19 NIV**

Blessings are on the head of the righteous, but violence covers the mouth of the wicked. **Proverbs 10:6 NKJV**

But for those who are self-seeking and who reject the truth and follow evil, there will be wrath and anger. **Romans 2:8 NIV**

The house of the wicked will be will be overthrown, But the tent of the upright will flourish. **Proverbs 14:11 NKJV**

The labor of the righteous leads to life, The wages of the wicked to sin. **Proverbs 10:7 KJV**

21 They gave me also gall for my meat; and in my thirst, they gave me vinegar to drink. **22** Let their table become a snare; that which should have been for their welfare, let it become a trap. **Psalm 69:21-22 KJV**

Affirmations to Fight Against My Enemies:

- ❖ As you do evil and selfish acts against me, I will keep my peace. The more and more you attack me, the greater my faith grows in God and in His word. You cannot, and you will not hurt me.
- ❖ I refuse to take revenge upon my enemies and jeopardize my life, my freedom, my integrity, my Godly character, my financial means, my health and my peace. I declare this in the name of Jesus.
- ❖ I am responsible for my own behavior and refuse to react foolishly toward the actions of my enemies because God will hold me accountable.
- ❖ I am a humble child of God and I do good to others. The more you attack me, the more God elevates me. You are defeated and cast down to the ground.
- ❖ I am the righteousness of God and blessings are on my head. You are filled with wickedness and deceit and violence.
- ❖ *I refuse to become a mockery and an embarrassment to my children and family I will not be provoked by the enemy, I will be still and allow God to fight my battles.
- ❖ I will allow his wrath to fall upon my enemies and avenge me despite my desire to act. I must, and I will, in the name of Jesus, be patient and wait on God.
- ❖ I am protected by the Lord. The arms you use to strike and cause me harm, will be broken by the Lord. I am the righteousness of God and He holds me up and keeps me safe.

- ❖ When you carry out your lies, betrayal, mistrust and wrong doings upon me, it angers God because I am His child.
- ❖ Your reckless and evil attempts to do evil upon me will return to you void. And Your life will be filled with rotten fruit because you have sowed rotten fruit upon my life.
- ❖ I am the righteousness of God and everything that God blesses in my life will flourish and multiply. Meanwhile, as you attempt to attack me, your evil house of lies and deceit will be overthrown and destroyed.
- ❖ When the enemy tries to destroy me by throwing rocks in secret, I will continue to operate as a child of God because He is my protector. He covers me all times.
- ❖ The more the enemy tries to attack me, the more I fall on my knees and fight with the word of God. I run to God and take refuge under his wings and watch His mighty wrath unveil.
- ❖ God is fair and righteous God. He is also a God of wrath to those who operate in evil. Therefore, I will do what is right despite the evil attacks of the enemy. I refuse to have the wrath of God upon my life.

CHAPTER 6

UNBREAKABLE -Heartache

Who dares to say that they have never suffered a broken heart? I find it safe to say, that at some point in our lives we all have experienced it. It can go as far back as junior high school where we called it puppy love or in high school, being dumped by a girlfriend or boyfriend may have been devastating and embarrassing. However, as adults and young adults, a severe heartache can not only be devastating but also debilitating. Some individuals fall into a depression. They withdraw themselves from family and friends. They cry constantly, sleep all day and lose weight due to loss of appetite. Some individuals even quit taking time to groom themselves as well.

In addition, a heartache can make it difficult to work or take care of your daily activities due to the inability to focus and/or the lack motivation. Depression caused from a broken heart can even lead to suicide. The feeling of rejection and not being good enough or valued can cause an individual to feel a sense of hopelessness as if they are not worthy of being loved nor deemed important. Getting professional help from a psychiatrist or therapist is strongly recommended to help deal with these feelings. Medication may also be necessary in some cases; but if you feel as if your life is going in a downward spiraling out of control, please seek help.

Moreover, in conjunction with mental health services, I do emphasize that there is miraculous healing in the word of God for heartache. God's word comforts us and reminds us that we are loved. We are his children and that He loved us so much, He gave up his only son for us to die on the cross for our salvation. God's word gives us strength, comfort and reassurance that no matter how bad it hurts, it will be alright in due time. It is truly a process. It is a transformation. It is a growth. Dealing with a loss or separation takes time to heal. It is not by far easy; but if you meditate on the word daily, you will find that you will eventually get stronger and stronger with each day that passes. Be consistent in the word and God will bring you comfort.

Scriptures for Heartache:

And you are complete in Him, who is the head of all principality and power. **Colossians 2:10 NKJV**

He heals the brokenhearted and binds up their wounds. **Psalms 147:33 NIV**

Cast all your anxiety on him because He cares for you **1 Peter 5:7 NIV**

And the peace of God, which transcends all understanding, will guard your hearts and your minds in Christ Jesus. **Philippians 4:7 NIV**

Above all else, guard your heart, for everything you do flows from it. **Proverbs 4:23 NIV**

The Lord gives strength to his people; the Lord blesses his people with peace. **Psalms 29:11 NIV**

I can do all thing in Christ who strengthens me. **Philippians 4:13 NIV**

You will keep in perfect peace those whose minds are steadfast because they trust in you. **Isaiah 26:3 NIV**

The Lord will keep you from harm. He will watch over your life. **Psalms 121:7 NIV**

6 Do not be anxious about anything, but in every situation, by prayer and petition, with thanksgiving, present your request to God. **7** And the peace of God, which transcends all understanding, will guard your hearts and minds in Christ Jesus. **Philippians 4:6-7 NIV**

Restore to me the joy of your salvation and grant me a willing spirit, to sustain me. **Psalm 51:12 NIV**

The rain came down, the streams rose, and the winds blew and beat against that house; yet it did not fall, because it had its foundation on the rock. **Matthew 7:25 NIV**

The Lord is my rock, my fortress and my deliverer. **2 Samuel 22:2 NIV**

The Lord is close to the brokenhearted and he saves those who are crushed in spirit. **Psalms 34:18 NIV**

Restore us, O God, make your face shine on us, that we may be saved. **Psalms 8:3 NIV**

But I trust in you, Lord; I say, "You are my God". **Psalm 31:14 NIV**

You will keep in perfect peace those whose minds are steadfast, because they trust in you. **Isaiah 26:3 NIV**

29 He gives strength to the weary and increases the power of the weak. **30** Even youth grow tired and weary, and young men stumble and fall; **31** but those who hope in the Lord will Renew their strength. They will soar on wings like eagles; they will run and not grow weary. They will walk and not faint. **Isaiah 40: 29-31 NIV**

Affirmations for the Brokenhearted:

- ❖ I am complete in Jesus who is the head of principalities and powers. I do not need acceptance or approval of anyone because I am whole through Christ Jesus.
- ❖ The Lord is healing my broken heart. As I trust him, He is removing the pain and the hurt.
- ❖ God nurtures my soul and binds my up wounds.
- ❖ I refuse to be consumed with worry, fear and sorrow. I cast out every negative thought and emotion and turn it over to God.
- ❖ My mind and heart will not be a manipulated by the lies of the enemy for all of my trust is in the Lord.
- ❖ I refuse to be a captive of pain and hurt. I will live a life of joy and happiness because God is my deliver.

- I use the wisdom of God and the spirit of discernment to guard and protect my heart from anyone who attempts to hurt me.
- I receive joy and peace through the word of God and his truth. God takes away all of my burdens and allow my mind and body to function with perfection in every way.
- Because God takes charge over all hurt and pain in my life, I am not distracted. I maintain my focus and direction. I care for my children, work efficiently and take care of my daily task with excellence every day.
- I surround myself with positive people who love me and care about my wellbeing. I do not isolate myself from those who encourage me but go out and enjoy life. Each day is a beautiful gift and I rejoice in it with laughter and with a joyful heart.
- No matter what trials I go through, I am never alone because God is by my side. He will never abandon me in my time of need. God loves me and He is forever present in my life.
- God keeps me in perfect peace because I keep my mind and my focus on him. Through meditation of the word, prayer and thanksgiving, all of my worries are cast down and my peace is restored.
- God watches over me day and night and he protects me from harm and heartache.
- God restores my strength. He gives me the power to soar in the sky like the eagles. I will not grow tired. My spirit, my mind and my heart are renewed. I have new life.

CHAPTER 7

UNBREAKABLE-Kin Folk-Family

Family...we are an extremely diverse group of people, from races to cultures to customs and traditions. We have a lot of diversities amongst us but whether we like it or not, we have more things in common than not. Sometimes we love our families and sometimes we hate them; Sometimes we can't get enough of them and other times we simply can't get far enough away from them. Some family members are very active in our lives, while others have no presence at all but regardless of all the facts, we all have a family somewhere.

Just like with the average everyday people we meet, with family, we must always be wise to operate in Godly order. Family are people that will, for the most part forever have ties to us. Therefore, setting boundaries, treating one another with love, respect and having routine fellowship are crucial elements in having a well-balanced family life.

Furthermore, the unit of family can be extremely complex. There are multiple components of a family that can operate in very different ways depending upon numerous things. As mentioned previously, we have cultural difference, we also have religious difference, differences in family infrastructure and family dynamics such as blended families, adoptions, extended families or even dysfunctional characteristics learned and passed down such as poor communication. However, despite all the things that can impact our family for good or bad, walking in Godly love will never go out of style.

Scriptures for Kin Folks: Family:

Now the Lord had said unto Abram, get thee out of thy country, and from thy kindred, and from thy father's house, unto a land that I will shew thee: 2And I will make of thee a great nation, and I will bless thee, and make thy name great; and thou shalt be a blessing: **Genesis 12:1-2 NIV**

When his brothers saw that their father loved him more than any of them, they hated him and could not speak a kind word to him. **Genesis 37:4 NIV**

The day for building your walls will come, the day for extending your boundaries. **Micah 7:11 NIV**

You set a boundary they cannot cross; never again will they cover the earth. **Psalm 104:9 NIV**

Do not move an ancient boundary stone set up by your ancestors. **Proverbs 22:28 NIV**

He is to share equally in their benefits even though he has received money from the sale of family possessions. **Deuteronomy 18:8 NIV**

Whoever brings ruin on their family will inherit only wind, and the fool will be servant to the wise. **Proverbs 11:29 NIV**

You will have plenty of goats' milk to feed your family and to nourish your female servants **Proverbs 27:27 NIV**

She gets while it is still night; she provides food for her family and portions for her female servants. **31:15 NIV**

If anyone does not know how to manage his own family, how can he take care of God's church? **1 Timothy 3:5 NIV**

This is the written account of Adam's family line. When God created mankind, he made them in the likeness of God. **Genesis 5:1 NIV**

The Lord then said to Noah, "Go into the ark, you and your whole family, because I have found you righteous in this generation. **Genesis 7:1 NIV**

They also failed to show any loyalty to the family of Jerub-Baal (that is, Gideon) in spite of all the good things he had done for them. **Judges 8:35 NIV**

But when you give to the needy, do not let your left hand know what your right hand is doing. **Matthew 6:3 NIV**

"In your anger do not sin"; Do not let the sun go down while you are still angry. **Ephesians 4:26 NIV**

Children, obey your parents in the Lord; for this is right **Ephesians 6:1 KJV**

Children, obey your parents in all things; for this is well pleasing unto the Lord. **Colossians 3:20 KJV**

"The eye that mock a father that scorns an aged mother, will be pecked out by the ravens of the valley, will be eaten by the vultures. **Proverbs 30:17 NIV**

Soft answer turns away wrath, but harsh word stirs up anger. **Proverbs 15:1 NIV**

Affirmation for Kinfolk: Family:

- ❖ At designated times I separate myself from my family and loved ones in order to hear from God and to allow him to reveal the unseen things of the spirit to me. By doing so and being obedient, He blesses me. God elevates me and makes me great. He allows me to be a blessing to others.
- ❖ I show the love of God to my siblings. I am not get jealous of them nor am I selfish. I am honest and trustworthy. I speak kind words to encourage and lift them up.
- ❖ I use the wisdom of God and create boundaries with my family in order to maintain a healthy and well-balanced relationship. My boundaries are clear, precise and consistent to prevent confusion and misunderstandings.
- ❖ My family is grounded in Christ. We respect the firm foundation and wisdom of our elders and ancestors before us which is rooted in the word of God. Christ is and always will be the center of my family.
- ❖ I help my family who are in need and rely on Godly discernment. I allow God to order my steps and direct my path concerning the way I provide help for my family.
- ❖ I am not overwhelmed and stressed by issues that affect my family due to their repeated disobedience to God and their foolish actions. Their emergency is not my emergency. I do not take on their burdens but cast the care on Christ Jesus, our Lord and Savior.

- ❖ I bring hope and prosperity to my family. I bring love and joy. I bring the word of God to uplift and to build up their faith in Christ. I do not do things to destroy or tear down my family; nor do I curse them or break their spirits, for this is not of God. The one who does this will have misery and their soul will never proper.
- ❖ God is blessing my family. He provides everything that we need. We will never thirst or hunger. He has above and beyond what we will ever need. God is our provider.
- ❖ As a Godly wife, mother and woman of the house I work diligently to care for my family. I work while my family sleeps in preparation for the next day. I provide nurturance for my family and see to it that all their needs are met.
- ❖ I must manage my own home first before I am adequately capable of managing in the house of God. Therefore, my house is in order. My family, my bills, my laundry, my closet, my dishes, my rooms, my yard, and my garage are all in order.
- ❖ Because God created man in his own image, my entire family is made in the image of God and his likeness. We possess the character of God and walk in Godly wisdom daily.
- ❖ Just as God protected Noah and his family from the flood for his obedience and faithfulness, God covers and protects my family from all hurt, harm and danger. *Noah was a righteous man and I declare that my family also is the righteousness of God.

- ❖ Yet, I am loyal and show love, I am not disheartened by the lack of loyalty shown to me by my family. I do what is right in the eyes of God and according to his word. I receive rewards from my God in heaven and not from man. I am the righteous of God and I continue to walk in love and do what is right.

- ❖ In helping family members, I do not make it public knowledge for the entire family to know. I give out of spiritual discernment and the direction of God.

- ❖ I resolve conflict in my family. I address issues of discord as soon as possible and do not allow anger to set in my spirit and fester.

- ❖ As an adult child, I love, respect and honor my parents. I see that they are properly cared for and have the necessary things they need, to the best of my ability, to live a comfortable life just as they did for me when I was a child. This is right and it pleases God.

- ❖ I take the care of my elderly parents seriously. I do not mock, scorn or take advantage of them but treat them with love, compassion and respect. By honoring my parents, I honor God. Those who do not honor their parents, your lives will be cursed.

- ❖ I avoid strife and family conflict by choosing my words with Godly wisdom. I respond with words that are not offensive and do not ignite anger. My words are filled with kindness, compassion and understanding.

CHAPTER 8

UNBREAKABLE- Forever Thankful

In life, we at times go through the motions from day to day without stepping back to say, "Thank you God. Thank you for giving us another day and allowing us to enjoy just the simple things." We take for granted so many things without realizing it; the beautiful sunshine, the soothing rain, the gentle breeze, and the sweet sounds of birds singing. We are so accustomed to having certain things, I call blessings, that we become complacent and comfortable with them. We are almost willing to bet that these hidden blessings will always remain with the opportunity of enjoying them over and over again. Most times we don't appreciate something until it is taken away from us. We may complain about our job until we are fired and then we realize just how important it really was because now we are unable to pay our mortgage. We may criticize our bodies and point out all the imperfections and idiosyncrasies until we become sick and our health is failing. We are all guilty of it. Did you know there is always someone out there less fortunate than you are and is praying for just an ounce of what you have?

Be thankful for where you are despite turmoil and trying situations. In the mist, yet and still, give God thanks. It could always be so much worse. Instead of looking at what we don't have, look at what we do have. Instead of focusing on what is wrong, focus on what is right. Stay mindful of how these things are blessings to our lives and how we in turn, use them to bless the lives of others. In everything that we have, give God all the praise and the glory. In everything that God provides us with, thank Him. He is a beautiful and an amazing God. He expects our praises of thanksgiving, it but most importantly, He deserves them.

Scriptures of Thanksgiving:

Come into his gates with thanksgiving, and into his courts with praise: be thankful unto him, and bless his name. **Psalms 100:4 KJV**

Devote yourselves to prayer, being watchful and thankful. **Colossians 4:2 NIV**

Therefore, since we are receiving a kingdom that cannot be shaken, let us be thankful, and so worship God acceptably with reverence and awe, **Hebrew 12:28**

May he give you the desire of your heart and make all your plans succeed. **Psalm 20:4 NIV**

That my heart may sing your praises and not be silent. Lord my God, I will praise you forever. **Psalm 30:12 NIV**

Give praise to the Lord, proclaim his name: make known among the nations what he has done. **Psalm 105:1 NIV**

Give thanks in all circumstances; for this is God's will for you in Christ Jesus 1**Thessalonians 5:18 NIV**

If I take part in the meal with thankfulness, why am I denounced because of something I thank God for? **1 Corinthians 10:30 NIV**

Sing to the Lord with grateful praise; make music to our God on the harp. **Psalm 147:7 NIV**

Whoever regards one day as special does so to the Lord. Whoever eats meat does so to the Lord, for they give thanks to God; and whoever abstains does so to the Lord and gives thanks to God. **Romans 14:6 NIV**

When you sacrifice a thank offering to the Lord, sacrifice it in such a way that it will be accepted on your behalf. **Leviticus 22:29 NIV**

They were also to stand every morning to thank and praise the Lord. They were to do the same in the evening. **1 Chronicles 29:13 NIV**

Then he took a cup, and when he had given thanks, he gave it to them, saying, Drink from it, all of you. **Matthew 26:27 NIV**

Immediately he stood up in front of them, took what he had been lying on and went home praising God. **Luke 5:25 NIV**

Immediately he received his sight and followed Jesus, praising God. When all the people saw it, they also praised God. **Luke 18:43**

"Return home and tell how much God has done for you". So, the man went away and told all over town how much Jesus had done for him. **Luke 8:39**

Jesus then took the loaves, gave thanks, and distributed to those who were seated as much as they wanted. He did the same with the fish. **John 6:11**

He jumped to his feet and began to walk. Then he went with them into the temple courts, walking and Jumping, and praising God. **Acts 3:8 NIV**

He threw himself at Jesus' feet and thanked him- and he was a Samaritan. **Luke 17:16 NIV**

So, they took away the stone. Then Jesus looked up and said, "Father, I thank you that you have heard me. **John 11:41**

Devote yourselves to prayer, being watchful and thankful. **Colossians 4:2 NIV**

Affirmations of Thanksgiving:

- ❖ I humbly approach God with thanksgiving upon my lips. I can never thank him enough for all that he has done in my life.
- ❖ I pray to God daily and wait with thanksgiving on my tongue. I am confident in his mighty power and I sit still knowing that God will work out the situation in his own timing and according to His will.

- ❖ Your love is so great and bountiful, Lord. I will never allow anyone to prevent me from giving thanks to You. You are a generous God and the rocks will not cry out for me.
- ❖ God has the supreme power over every situation and circumstance over my life. He is the first and the last; and because of this, I am forever grateful for His covering over me.
- ❖ I have a loving and mighty Father in God. I am thankful that God looks out for my wellbeing and takes care of my every need despite what a situation may look like. He gives me the desires of my heart as it aligns with his words. I am always victorious because He loves me and gives me abundant life.
- ❖ My Lord overwhelms me with His excellence, His grace and His mercy time and time again. I am gracious for to Him and I will live a life giving Him total honor, praise and glory.
- ❖ I will shout God's praises to the world. I am not ashamed to acknowledge His grace and mercy over my life. He rescued me from the pit of hell. God is my Redeemer and my deliver. He is my Savior.
- ❖ Despite this diagnosis, I still praise your name. You are my healer and I am thankful. According to your words, by your stripes, I am healed and you are not a God that you would lie.
- ❖ Although my marriage appears to be in trouble, I give you the praise in the mist of my troubles because you are a redeemer; for your word says that what God has put together let no man put asunder.

- Although my child is disobedient and unruly, I praise You Lord and I am thankful for Your guidance. I have set a solid foundation for him in the word of God. I have trained him according to Your teachings. I rejoice and give You the glory because Your word is deeply imbedded within his heart and he will never depart from it.
- My desire is to please God therefore, I give Him my very best because He gives me His best. God is my Father and my Provider. I delight myself in Him and He gives me the desires of my heart.
- I praise God at all times. My heart overflows with thanksgiving. I cry out with praise in the morning, noon day and at night. I can never praise Him enough for all that He has done for me. I will bless Him at all times.
- I am appreciative at all times. Everything that the Lord has given to me, I am thankful. I know that I am blessed and that there is someone in a far worse predicament. I thank God for always keeping me, lifting me up and covering my family.

CHAPTER 9

UNBREAKABLE- Betrayal or Loyalty

Who has been betrayed? Or better yet, who has not been betrayed? I feel that I can go on record and say that at some point in time in your life you have experienced some type of betrayal one way or another. It may have been a sister or brother; a husband or wife, a son or daughter, a dear friend or even a mother or father. Betrayal…I can honestly say that this may be one of the most hurtful and agonizing encounters that a person may face in their lifetime. I say this because of the trust factor. When a person trusts, they let their guards down. They allow you into the most intimate setting that they have. They share their true thoughts. They share their heart, emotions, personal space, friendship, loyalty and trust that you will take care of it.

Furthermore, when a person trusts, they are essentially naked. When you are naked you are stripped bare; exposed to the elements leaving you completely vulnerable. Vulnerable to the fear of judgement, by opening up and exposing the "real" you. They have faith that you will not hurt them but protect them and keep them safe. How emotionally devastating this can be to learn that the person you trusted with all your precious and intimate details did not have your best interest at heart. Thank God for His grace and mercy. He knows all and He feels our pain and hurt. God's word gives us insight and wisdom on how to deal with such individuals and how to maintain our Godly character. Yes, it can be difficult but just like everything else, God will equip us with the tools to walk away victorious.

Scriptures of Betrayal and Loyalty:

Surely such is the dwelling of an evil man; such is the place of one who does not know God." **Job 18:21 NIV**

That the mirth of the wicked is brief, the joy of the godless lasts but a moment. **Job 20:5 NIV**

He preserveth not the life of the wicked: but giveth right to the poor. **Job 36:6 KJV**

The wages of the righteous is life, but the earnings pf the wicked are sin and death. **Proverbs 10:16 NIV**

Peter declared, "Even if all fall away, I will not.". **Mark 14:29 NIV**

I do not base my friendship

At that time many will turn away from the faith and will betray and hate each other. **Matthew 24:10 NIV**

Will he thank the servant because he did what he was told to do? **Luke 17:9 NIV**

They risked their lives for me. Not only I but all the churches of the Gentiles are grateful to them. **Romans 16:4 NIV**

I have not stopped giving thanks for you, remembering you in my prayers. **Ephesians 1:16 NIV**

I thank my God every time I remember you. **Philippians 1:3 NIV**

Return their cloak by sunset so that your neighbor may sleep in it. Then they will thank you, and it will be regarded as a righteous act in the sight of the Lord you God. **Deuteronomy 24:13 NIV**

A man that hath friends must shew himself friendly: and there is a friend that sticketh closer than a brother. **Proverbs 18:24 KJV**

Do this now, my son, and deliver thyself, when thou art come into the hand of thy friend: go, humble thyself, and make sure thy friend. **Proverbs 6:3 KJV**

My friends scorn me: but mine eye poureth out tears unto God. **Job 16:20**

If anyone denounces their friends for reward, the eyes of their children will fail. **Job 17:5**

All my intimate friends detest me; those I love have turned against me. **Job 19:19 NIV**

It is a sin to despise one's neighbor, but blessed is the one who is kind to the needy. **Proverbs 14:21 NIV**

Iron sharpens iron; so, one person sharpens another. **Proverb 27:17 NIV**

Perfume and incense bring joy to the heart, and the pleasantness of a friend springs from their heartfelt advice. **Proverbs 27:9 NIV**

Affirmations for Betrayal or Loyalty:

- ❖ I have an intimate relationship with God and I walk with Godly character. I do what is right according to His word. If I should fall short, I repent and ask for forgiveness because evil has no place in my heart nor in the kingdom of God.
- ❖ Yet I have been betrayed, I continue to walk in love. I am not tainted by the evil acts of others for their joy is brief and only temporary.
- ❖ While God saves me from those who attempt to destroy my life through their wicked acts; the wicked brings death, hardship and turmoil to their own lives through their evil actions.
- ❖ I am the righteousness of God. I am blessed with a life of joy and peace meanwhile the wicked is cursed with death.
- ❖ I do not scorn my friends but show love and kindness. If I have a disagreement with my friend I seek God for guidance and wisdom to resolve it.
- ❖ I show loyalty to my friends. I do not sacrifice our friendship for material things. I give friendship and receive friendship out of genuine love and respect.
- ❖ I show kindness and the love of God to my friends and those who are in need.

CHAPTER 10

UNBREAKABLE – The Lost

Life sometimes throws us curve balls that we never see coming. It can be the result of the loss of a job, divorce, a broken vehicle, a death, a sickness or even a catastrophic event such as losing a home to a fire or a hurricane. These situations can immediately put us in a state of panic. We get confused, frustrated and stressed out trying to figure out what in the world to do. It is understandable why one might be in a tail spin. The unexpected circumstance can put us in a state of shock and confusion. We need Godly wisdom, direction and guidance. We are also in need of his protection. When we are faced with crisis we often feel lost. It is like someone dropped you in the abyss of the cold, dark ocean. You can't see; you can't breathe and you are fighting to find your way to the surface for air. You are vulnerable to the elements and any neighboring predators that may be lurking (those who sit back and wait in judgement to see how deep you sink). At this point, we tend to fall back on what we know best, our own wisdom. Unfortunately, several of us try to resolve issues ourselves without seeking guidance from God.

Furthermore, there are situations where we choose certain paths for our lives deliberately, with no desire or intent to consult God first. It is likely that we choose certain paths and make certain decisions from operating out of our flesh. We consciously walk in disobedience knowingly and willingly. When we operate from the flesh, we risk forming new habits that are in direct disobedience to God. These habits have the potential to create massive storms in your life. They may make you lose your job, cause a divorce, create sickness, create financial hardship and destroy lives. Nothing good can come from disobedience to God. Eventually, over a period of time, you are revealed. You are left hurting and confused not knowing which way to turn, what to do or how to find our way out. You are lost.

Consequently, the word of God has a remedy for lost souls; those who are in crisis, and experiencing despair and confusion. Those who have made poor decisions and have purposely disobeyed God. God has the power to do all things. He can restore us and make our situation work in our favor according to His will for our lives. We must seek Godly wisdom and guidance and God can lead us back on the path of righteousness, peace and joy.

Scriptures for Wisdom for the Lost:

For the Son of Man came to seek and to save the lost. **Luke 19:10 NIV**

And if he finds it, truly I tell you, he is happier about that one sheep than about the ninety-nine that did not wander off. **Matthew 18:13 NIV**

Wisdom is the principal thing: therefore, get wisdom: and with all thy getting get understanding. **Proverbs 4:7 KJV**

For wisdom is a defence, and money is a defence: but the excellency of knowledge is, that wisdom giveth life to them that have it. **Ecclesiastes 7:12 KJV**

The fear of the Lord is the beginning of knowledge: but fools despise wisdom and instruction. **Proverb 1:7 KJV**

King Solomon exceeded all the kings of the earth for riches and for wisdom. **1 King 10:23 KJV**

O that ye would altogether hold your peace! And it should be your wisdom. **Job 13:5 KJV**

My mouth shall speak of wisdom; and the meditation of my heart shall be of understanding. **Psalms 49:3 KJV**

To him that by wisdom made the heavens: for his mercy endureth forever. **Psalms 136:5 KJV**

To know wisdom and instruction; to perceive the words of understanding; **Proverbs 1:2 KJV**

So that thou incline thine ear unto wisdom, and apply thine heart to understanding; **Proverb 2:2 KJV**

I incline my ears to the word of God and I receive wisdom; For the Lord giveth wisdom: out of his mouth cometh knowledge and understanding. **Proverbs 2:6 KJV**

Happy is the man that findeth wisdom, and the man that getteth understanding. **Proverbs 3:13 KJV**

The Lord by wisdom hath founded the earth; by understanding hath he established the heavens. **Proverbs 3:19 KJV**

My son, let not them depart from thine eyes: keep sound wisdom and discretion **Proverbs 3:21 KJV**

Get wisdom, get understanding: forget it not; neither decline from the words of my mouth. **Proverbs 4:5 KJV**

I have taught thee in the way of wisdom; I have led thee in right paths. **Proverbs 4:11 KJV**

Counsel is mine, and sound wisdom: I am understanding; I have strength. **Proverbs 8:14 KJV**

The lips of the righteous feed many: but fools die for want of wisdom. **Proverbs 10:21 KJV**

The mouth of the just bringeth forth wisdom: but the forward tongue shall be cut out. **Proverbs 10:31 KJV**

When pride cometh, then cometh shame: but with the lowly is wisdom. **Proverbs 11:2 KJV**

Only by pride cometh contention: but with the well advised is wisdom. **Proverbs 13:10 KJV**

A scorner seeketh wisdom, and findeth it not: but knowledge is easy unto him that understandeth. **Proverbs 14:6 KJV**

The fear of the Lord is the instruction of wisdom: and before honour is humility. **Proverbs 15:33 KJV**

Through desire a man, having separated himself, seeketh and intermeddleth with all wisdom. **Proverbs 18:1 KJV**

He that getteth wisdom loveth his own soul: he that keepepth understanding shall find good. **Proverbs 19:8 KJV**

Through wisdom is a house build; and by understanding it is established **Proverbs 24:3 KJV**

Wisdom is too high for a fool: he openeth not his mouth in the gate. **Proverbs 24:7 KJV**

Whoso loveth wisdom rejoiceth his father. But he that keepeth company with harlots spendeth his substance. **Proverbs 29:3 KJV**

My son, do not let wisdom and understanding out of your sight, preserve sound judgment and discretion; **Proverbs 3:21 NIV**

Do not forsake wisdom, and she will protect you; love her, and she will watch over you. **Proverbs 4:6 NIV**

If you are wise, your wisdom will reward you: if you are a mocker, you alone will suffer. **Proverbs 9:12 NIV**

From the mouth of the righteous comes the fruit of wisdom, but a perverse tongue will be silenced. **Proverbs 10:31 NIV**

The wisdom of the prudent is to give thought to their ways, but the folly of fools is deception. **Proverbs 14:8 NIV**

Why should fools have money in hand to buy wisdom, when they are not able to understand it? **Proverbs 17:16 NIV**

Where there is no revelation, people cast off restraint; but blessed is the one who heeds wisdom's instruction. **Proverbs 29:18 NIV**

By your wisdom and understanding you have gained wealth for yourself and amassed gold and silver in your treasuries. **Ezekiel 28:4 NIV**

For I will give you words and wisdom that none of your adversaries will be able to resist or contradict. **Luke 21:15 NIV**

For the foolishness of God is wiser than human wisdom, and the weakness of God is stronger than human strength. **1 Corinthians 1:25 NIV**.

If any of you lack wisdom, you should ask God, who gives generously to all without finding fault, and it will be given to you. **James 1:5 NIV**

Unbreakable

Affirmations of Wisdom for the Lost:

- God finds me and rescues me from all doubts and concerns.
- Should I ever become lost and lose my way, God shall find me and return me to His flock amongst all of His children. He is overjoyed that I am once again safe from harm.
- I seek the word of God daily to obtain wisdom. As I obtain wisdom, I receive a clearer understanding of my life and its direction according to God.
- I have the wisdom of God and His wisdom of gives me life to conquer all things.
- I reverence the lord and seek to gain Godly wisdom, knowledge and understanding therefore, I do not waste time arguing with unbelievers who refuses the direction of Christ for a fool despises Godly wisdom and instruction.
- Such as King Solomon, I am exceedingly blessed with riches and wisdom.
- I am wise because I hold my peace. I do not operate and speak recklessly out of my emotions.
- As I meditate daily I get understanding which allows me to speak and operate with wisdom as I move throughout my day and interact with others.
- God knows all things and has the wisdom and compassion to resolves all issues of my life. He is merciful, and I am covered in his protection and wisdom.

- ❖ I receive counsel from my Lord and I am equipped with wisdom, understanding and strength to conquer any obstacle. With God's wisdom, I am strong and undefeated.
- ❖ The more I read and study the word of God, the wiser I become and the greater I understand God's instruction for my life.
- ❖ I receive all wisdom, guidance and understanding from the Lord. I am equipped to handle any situation with grace, integrity and character.
- ❖ I have the wisdom of God to bless those in need as God directs me to do.
- ❖ I walk in humility and wisdom. I do not walk in pride because it brings about shame.
- ❖ I fear the Lord and He instructs me with wisdom. I operate in humility and the Lord honors me. He blesses me with favor daily.
- ❖ I am in full of peace and joy because I have the wisdom of God which give me understanding in my life.
- ❖ I separate myself from the outside world and commune with God daily to seek wisdom to direct my path.
- ❖ I love my soul therefore and I seek to feed it Godly wisdom daily. Wisdom gives me understanding and helps my life to be fruitful.
- ❖ I build my house and foundation on the wisdom of God. I maintain my foundation by understanding the wisdom that the Lord reveals to me through daily meditation.

- ❖ I honor, love and respect the wisdom of God. I never take it for granted for it protects and watches over me all my days.
- ❖ Because I have the wisdom of God I am rewarded with good things; unlike the mocker who will be alone and filled with despair and trouble.
- ❖ I am consumed with the wisdom of God. It pumps through every vein, artery and blood vessel in my body. It allows me to take thought and caution to all my actions and behaviors.
- ❖ I am financially stable. I have all the provisions I need to support my family. I am blessed above and beyond with riches and treasures because God has given me the wisdom to get wealth.
- ❖ I keep Godly wisdom and understanding in my sight at all times. I preserve sound judgment and discretion when I make crucial decisions in my life and the lives of my children.

Scriptures for Guidance for the Lost:

The meek will he guide in judgement: and the meek will he teach his way. **Psalms 25:9 NIV**

Teach me thy way, O Lord, and lead me in a plain path, because of mine enemies. **27:11 Psalms KJV**

Lead me, O Lord, in thy righteousness because of mine enemies; make thy way straight before my face. **Psalms 5:8 KJV**

And I will bring the blinds by a way that they knew not; I will lead them in paths that they have not known: I will make darkness light before them, and crooked things straight. These things will I do unto them, and not forsake them. **Isaiah 42:16 KJV**

And it shall be, that thou shalt drink of the brook; and I have commanded the ravens to feed thee there. **1 Kings 17:4 KJV**

Lead me in thy truth, and teach me: for thou art the God of my salvation; on thee do I wait all the day. **Psalms 25:5 KJV**

A person's steps are directed by the Lord. How then can anyone understand their own way? **Proverbs 20:24 NIV**

I will instruct thee and teach thee in the way which thou shalt go: I will guide thee with mine eyes. **Psalms 32:8 KJV**

Even there shall thy hand lead me, and thy right hand shall hold me. **Psalms 139:10 KJV**

He maketh me to lie down in green pastures: he leadeth me beside the still waters. **Psalms 23:2 KJV**

And when he putteth forth his own sheep, he goeth before them, and the sheep follow him: for they know his voice. **John 10:4 KJV**

Hear instruction, and be wise, and refuse it not. **Proverbs 8:33 KJV**

And the Lord went before them by day in a pillar of a cloud, to lead them the way; and by night in a pillar of fire, to give them light; to go by day and night: **Exodus 13:21 KJV**

And thou shalt remember all the way which the Lord thy God led thee these forty years in the wilderness, to humble thee and to prove thee, to know what was in thine heart, whether thou wouldest keep his commandments, or no. **Deut 8:2 KJV**

For the Lord knoweth the way of the righteous: but the way of the ungodly shall peri sh. **Psalms 1:6 KJV**

The way of the wicked is like deep darkness; they do not know what makes them stumble. **Proverbs 4:19 NIV**

Where no counsel is, the people fall: but in the multitude of counsellors there is safety. **Proverbs 11:14 KJV**

Blessed is the man that walketh not in the counsel of the ungodly, nor standeth in the way of sinners, nor sitteth in the seat of the scornful. **Psalms 1:1 KJV**

The way of a fool is right in his own eyes: but he that hearkenth unto counsel is wise. **Proverbs 12:15 KJV**

Affirmations of Guidance:

*I am meek in spirit and allow myself to be guided by the Lord. I will learn all of His ways to maintain on the path of righteousness.

- ❖ The Lord teaches me and leads me in a clear path of understanding for my life. He keeps harm away from me.
- ❖ My God will lead me down a safe path and protect me from my enemies and any situations that may cause me harm.
- ❖ God will open my eyes so that I will see what is right. He will take me out of darkness and lead me into the light. He will

make my crooked ungodly ways straight and put me on the path of righteousness. He will never leave or forsake me.

- ❖ God loves me and will never forsake me. When I am troubled and lost, his hand leads me to solid ground and His right hand holds me up, steady and firm so I will not fall.
- ❖ I am God's sheep. He goes before me and guides my every step. I study the word daily and it takes root in my spirit. I follow God just as a child follows his mother and father for He is my father and I know His voice.
- ❖ All of my needs are met and I lack nothing. God leads and guides me to every resource that I need. He directs others to me with gifts and talents to meet my needs.
- ❖ The Lord leads and guides me in truth. He teaches me what is right. My God protects me from all dangers and heals my mind of all worries. I wait on the Lord because He is my Savior and have all power in His hands to transform any situation.
- ❖ My steps are ordered by the Lord. He is the Alpha and the Omega, the beginning and the end. It is impossible for me to guide my own way therefore, I trust God to lead my life.
- ❖ I listen to God and follow His direction for my life. I trust His guidance and His plans because He protects me and He loves me. God wants the very best for my life. He has plans for me to prosper.
- ❖ I continue to walk as a child of the Most High God even as I go through trying times. During these times, I learn to be humble

as I trust God and hide his words in my heart. I operate according to His word and honor His commandments.

- ❖ When the world is full of chaos and trouble, I seek comfort in God. He makes me lay down and rest in his presence. It is like a beautiful field of sweet green grass. His peace is like the lullaby of a gentle stream. My soul is comforted, my burdens are removed and I have peace.
- ❖ I am surrounded by wise counsel. I fellowship with believers and receive teaching from God's shepherd. He leads his sheep in spirit and truth. I am safe under the teachings of God's word for without wise counsel, the people fall.
- ❖ I am the righteousness of God and He knows my ways and guides me. I have a life of victory and produce good fruits.
- ❖ I am a child of God and I am a reflection of Him therefore, I am cautious of my affiliations and associations and actions.
- ❖ I follow God and He orders my steps. I have life and prosperity. I will not be destroyed nor will I perish because I am an obedient child of God.
- ❖ As I follow God, I walk in light. My way is clear and my path is straight. I do not stumble or fall because God is directing my every step.
- ❖ The wicked do not follow God, but Satan. They walk in darkness and are confused. Their lips rattle foolishness and are surrounded by chaos. They are so disoriented and cannot find their way. They become reckless and crash.

Unbreakable

Scriptures of Protection:

The righteous person may have many trouble. But the Lord delivers him from them all; he protects all his bones not one of them will be broken. **Psalm 34:19-20 NIV**

22The Jesus said to his disciples: "Therefore I tell you, do not worry about your life, what you will eat; or about, what you will wear. 23For life is more than food, and the body more than clothes. 24Consider the ravens: They do not sow or reap, they have no storeroom or barn; yet God feeds them. And how much more valuable you are than birds! 25Who of you by worrying can add a single hour to your life? **Luke 12:22-25 NIV**

3Surely he shall deliver thee from the snare of the fowler, and from the noisome pestilence. 4He shall cover thee with his feathers, and under his wings shalt thou trust: his truth shall be thy shield and buckler. **Psalms 91:3-4**

The Lord also will be a refuge for be oppressed, a refuge in times of trouble. **Psalms 9:9 KJV**

I laid me down and slept; I awaked; for the Lord sustained me. **Psalms 3:5 KJV**

The Lord preserveth all them that love him: but all the wicked will he destroy. **Psalms 145:20 KJV**

Hold up my goings in thy path, that my footsteps slip not. **Psalms 17:5 KJV**

Though he falls, he shall not be utterly cast down: for the Lord upholdeth him with his hand. **Psalms 37:24 KJV**

I will love thee, O Lord, my strength. **Psalms 18:1 KJV**

For he shall deliver the needy when he crieth; the poor also, and him that hath no helper. **Psalms 72:12 KJV**

Surely, he shall deliver thee from the snare of the fowler, and from the noisome pestilence. **Psalms 91:3 KJV**

Affirmations of Protection:

- ❖ I will not be worried about my life. Jesus provides everything that I need to live an abundant life. I have food, I have shelter, I have clothing. I want for nothing.
- ❖ I have faith in the almighty God. He protects me from harm day and night. My father delivers me out of hardship and trouble and I cast all my cares on Him. He never fails.
- ❖ When the enemy tries to attack me, God shields me under his wings and I cannot be touched. I trust God and he keeps me save from danger, seen and unseen.
- ❖ When I am in trouble. I seek God for his protection. He is my shield and my safe house. My place of peace.
- ❖ I have peace because God sustains and keeps me. I can rest without worry. I cast all my care on God because He cares for me.
- ❖ My steps are ordered by God and His guidance keeps my feet steady. I do not stumble or fall.

- ❖ God keeps and protects me in all my ways because I love Him and He recognizes me because I am His child. As for the wicked, they will be destroyed.
- ❖ Although I may stumble, I will not fall because the Lord holds me up with His hands.
- ❖ I love you Lord you are my strength in battle. I am more than a conqueror.
- ❖ When I am in need, God is by my side. When I cry, He comforts me. When I am in financial hardship, He delivers me. When I need help, He helps me.
- ❖ God is my means of deliverance in a time of trouble. He lets nothing harm me because He is God.
- ❖ Despite stress, frustration, financial burdens or pain I experience in life, I will be patient and wait on the Lord for He will deliver me completely. I will not be harmed, hurt or injured. Not one head on my head will be harmed nor one bone in my body be broken because I am the righteousness of God.

Unbreakable

CHAPTER 11

UNBREAKABLE- Self-Control

When we wake up each day, we never know what we will face. Indeed, we make short term goals such as: appointments scheduled weeks in advance, a to do list we may have the night before or perhaps a lunch date set or that afternoon. Furthermore, we also make long term goals for our lives involving our employment, our education, health, family, financial security and so on. But what happens if those plans are interrupted? Suppose suddenly you lost your job and now your family is in a financial crisis? Or perhaps a member of your immediate family was diagnosed with a devastating illness? How about a family experiencing a divorce? How would these traumatic experiences affect your daily life? What type of impact would it have on you? Would you be able to function effectively? Each individual handle situation differently, which can be attributed to how they were raised or their life experiences over the years. Some may slip into a depression while others may become very angry and be filled with rage. Regardless of how you cope with it one thing for certain is that you will be filled with emotion.

Fear, anger, worry, sorrow and envy are very common emotions we all face when dealing with monumental, unexpected situations in our lives. However, the word of God comforts us in all situations. We must not let these situations overtake our lives. We must continue to live. We must continue to press on. Just because we lost our job doesn't mean we stop caring for our children. They still need their parents to make sure they make it to school. They still need to eat breakfast in the morning. They still need help with homework. They still need to see you smiling and carrying on as usual. Just because you are going through a divorce it doesn't mean you quit your job. You still must go to work and perform with efficiency. In other words, the world continues to go on despite your situation. We must gain control of our emotions and continue to press on as God heals us through his word. Gain self-control by remembering what God has promised you. With each day of meditation, you gain strength in your spirit to move forward, to gain encouragement, to gain clarity and to eventually gain wholeness and healing in spirit through Christ Jesus.

Scriptures for Fear:

So, do not fear, for I am with you; do not be dismayed for I am your God. I will strengthen you and help you; I will uphold you with my righteous right hand. Isaiah **41:10 NIV**

Be strong and courageous. Do not be afraid or terrified because of them, for the Lord your God goes with you; he will never leave you nor forsake you. **Deuteronomy 31:6 NIV**

There is no fear in love; but perfect love casteth out fear; because fear hath torment. He that feareth is not made perfect in love. **1 John 4:18 KJV**

For God hath not given us the spirit of fear; but of power, and of love, and of a sound mind. **2 Timothy 1:7 KJV**

When I am afraid, I put my trust in you. **Psalms 56:3 NIV**

The Lord is on my side; I will not fear: what can man do unto me? **Psalms 118:6 KJV**

Ye shall not fear them: for the Lord your God he shall fight for you. **Deuteronomy 3:22 KJV**

Yea, though I walk through the valley of the shadow of death, I will fear no evil: for thou art with me; they rod and thy staff they comfort me. **Psalms 23:4 NIV**

What shall we then say to these things? If God be for us, who can be against us? **Romans 8:31 KJV**

Therefore, do not worry about tomorrow, for tomorrow will worry about itself. Each day has enough trouble of its own. **Matthew 6: 34 NIV**

I sought the Lord, and he heard me, and delivered me form all my fears. **Psalms 34:4 NIV**

Hear my voice, O God, in my prayer; preserve my life from fear of the enemy. **Psalms 64:1 NIV**

But whoso hearkenth unto me shall dwell safely, and shall be quiet from fear of evil. **Proverbs 1:33 KJV**

25 Have no fear of sudden disaster or of the ruin that overtakes the wicked, 26 for the Lord will be at your side and will keep your foot from being snared. **Proverbs 3:25-26 NIV**

Fear not, O land; be glad and rejoice; for the Lord will do great things. **Joel 2:21 KJV**

Fear not, little flock; for it is your Father's good pleasure to give you the kingdom. **Luke 12:32 NIV**

And I was with you in weakness, and in fear, and in much trembling. **1 Corinthians 2:3 NIV**

Fear ye not therefore, ye are of more value than many sparrows. **Matthew 10:31 KJV**

The fear if man bringeth a snare: but whoso putteth his trust in the Lord shall be safe. **Proverbs 29:25 KJV**

Affirmations for Fear:

- ❖ I am not afraid nor am I disheartened for God is with me. He strengthens me and helps me in my time need. My God holds me up and keeps me steady with his righteous hand so that I may not fall in times of trouble.

- ❖ I am strong and courageous. I am not fearful of anyone or anything. The Lord is with me at all time and He will never leave or forsake me.
- ❖ God is love and there is no fear in love. His love is perfect and removes all fear from my life. I am made perfect in the love of God and I walk in boldness and confidence.
- ❖ I do not fear because God has not given me the spirit of fear. God has equipped me with power, love and a clear mind to make intelligent and sound decisions concerning my life.
- ❖ Whenever fear attempts to invade my spirit, I put my complete trust in God and He delivers and strengthens me.
- ❖ As I go through my toughest storms and trials of life, I am not alone. God is there at all times. I do not fear because He surrounds me with a shield of protection. He sooths and comforts my mind, body and spirit and keeps me at peace.
- ❖ I cry to God and He hears my cry. God delivers me from all my fears, pain and anguish.
- ❖ God is with me so who dare choose to challenge Him? God will never be defeated, and I have victory in Jesus' name over every situation that attempts to disrupt my life.
- ❖ I do not worry about tomorrow. God and I deal with life one day at a time. Tomorrow has not yet arrived and it will have its own challenges. I trust God and allow Him to take control of every situation that concerns my life and accept that it will be in His own timing.

- ❖ When I pray to God He answers me. He saves and delivers me from the fear of those who try to attack me. I am safe and protected and cannot be touched.
- ❖ I am obedient to the word of God and He keeps me safe. I do not fear my enemies because God protects me in every situation.
- ❖ God provides for all of His creation; and If He watches over the sparrows of the sky, and my value is far greater, I have no fear that He will provide for me over and beyond.
- ❖ I do not fear sudden disaster or wicked acts of the enemy because God is at my side. He prevents my foot from getting tangled and prevents me from falling.
- ❖ I have joy and peace and I do not fear. The Lord continues to do marvelous works in my life daily and I am completely covered from the crown of my head to the soles of my feet.
- ❖ God desires to give me the kingdom and I have no reason to fear anything for He always provides for his children.
- ❖ For when I am in weakness, fear and trembling, I am never alone. God is there. He is right by my side building me up and giving me hope and strength to persevere.
- ❖ I refuse to allow fear to create disruption in my life. I put all my trust in the Lord who orders my steps. He covers me and keeps my family safe.

*What can man do to me? I cannot be touched, I have the covering of God on my life. He keeps me and protects me! I have the victory in Jesus' name!

Scriptures for Anger:

Refrain from anger and turn from wrath: do not fret-it leads only to evil. **37:8 NIV**

Don't say, "I'll pay you back for this wrong! "Wait for the Lord, and he will avenge you. **Proverbs 20:22 NIV**

The Lord is merciful and gracious, slow to anger, and plenteous in mercy. **Psalms 103:8 KJV**

A soft answer turneth away wrath: but grievous words stir up anger. **Proverbs 15:1 KJV**

A wrathful man stirreth up strife: but he that is slow to anger appeaseth strife. Proverbs **15:18 NIV**

Whoever sows injustice reaps calamity, and the rod they wield in fury will be broken. **Proverbs 22:8 NIV**

Let all bitterness, and wrath, and anger, and Lamour, and evil speaking, be put away from you, with all malice. **Ephesians 4:31 NIV**

Thou hast taken away all thy wrath: thou hast turned thyself from the fierceness of thine anger. **Psalms 85:3 KJV**

A person's wisdom yields patience; it is to one's glory to overlook an offense. **Proverbs 19:11 NIV**

Do not be quickly provoked in your spirit, for anger resides in the lap of fools. **Ecclesiastes 7:9 NIV**

But now ye also put off all these; anger, wrath, malice, blasphemy, filthy communication out of your mouth. **Colossians 3:8 KJV**

Cursed be their anger, for it was fierce; and their wrath, for it was cruel: I will divide them in Jacob, and scatter them in Israel. **Genesis 49:7 NIV**

Another dies in bitterness of soul, never having enjoyed anything good. **Job 21:25 NIV**

But the tongue can no man tame: it is an unruly evil, full of deadly poison. **James 3:8 KJV**

Let brotherly love continue. **Hebrews 13:1 KJV**

Love worketh no ill to his neighbor: therefore, love is the fulfilling of the law. **Romans 13:10 KJV**

Hatred stirreth up strife: but love covereth all sins **Proverbs 10:12 KJV**

But if ye do not forgive, neither will your Father which is in heaven forgive your trespasses. **Mark 11:26 KJV**

A new commandment I give unto you, that ye love on another; as I have loved you that ye also love one another. **John 13:34 KJV**

Dear friends, let us love one another, for love comes from God. Everyone who loves has been born of God and knows God. 8 Whoever does not love does not know God, because God is love. **1 John 4:7 NIV**

And let us not be weary in well doing: for in due season we shall reap, if we faint not. **Galatians 6:9 KJV**

22 But the fruit of the spirit is love, joy, peace, forbearance, kindness, goodness, faithfulness, 23 gentleness and self-control. Against such things there is no law. **Galatians 5:22-23 NIV**

Affirmations for Anger:

- ❖ I avoid anger and hostile situations because it will only leave to evil.
- ❖ The Lord is merciful, gracious and slow to anger and I have the character of the Lord.
- ❖ I avoid situations of anger, discord and confusion by selecting positive and uplifting words. I give responses of love, peace and understanding that defuse anger. I use Godly wisdom.
- ❖ I am in control of my behavior. I do not let anger dictate my actions. I am slow to anger, I bring about calmness and ease to an argumentative situation.
- ❖ I do not sow anger but love and peace and I reap the rewards of the kingdom.
- ❖ I avoid all gossip, complaining, bitterness, hate and anger. I operate with the wisdom of God and seek those actions that will bring joy, love and peace to my life and the lives of others.
- ❖ I remove anger from my heart and replace it with love so that I may be free.

- ❖ I have the wisdom of God and I am equipped to overlook offense. I am not easy annoyed but have patience to deal with the actions others in love.
- ❖ I cover sin with love. I do not judge but use the love of God to bring about peace. I rely on the strength of God to equip me to walk in love and to do what is right according to his word.
- ❖ I am not easily provoked or angered. I am in control of my emotions. I am patient and operate with the wisdom of God.
- ❖ I will not let corrupt communication proceed out of my mouth. I will speak words of faith, hope, love, compassion and joy daily to elevate my spirit and the spirit of others.
- ❖ I use love and compassion to bring about unity and understanding to troublesome situations.
- ❖ I enjoy life to the fullest. I have a merry heart and my soul is full of joy and the love of God.
- ❖ I am cautious of the words I speak. My tongue is a tremendous blessing and I have the power to speak life and healing into any situation.
- ❖ I walk in love with my brothers regardless of his actions. I am accountable to God for how I treat others and I allow God to deal with my brothers according to His will.
- ❖ I forgive others for their sins against me; by doing so, God forgives my sins. Therefore, when I am wrong and made angry, I forgive my brother in order to bring about peace and to show the love of God.

- ❖ I love my neighbor therefore I do not do evil towards them. I fulfill the love of God by loving my neighbor as myself.
- ❖ I am not angered by my brother but in fact, I love him. I love him as God has loves me.
- ❖ I love my brother because love comes from God; and because God is in me, I am made to love for God is love.
- ❖ I do not get angry or tired for doing what is right in the eyes of the Lord; for I know that if I do not give up, I will reap the blessings of God. I will stay strong and continue to press forward in Jesus' name.
- ❖ I am filled with overflowing love, joy, peace, forbearance, kindness, goodness, faithfulness, gentleness and self-control. Bitterness, anger and strife has no place in my life. I have the character of Christ and my spirit is filled with the fruit of the spirit.

Scriptures for Worry & Anxiety:

Why, my soul, are you downcast? Why so disturbed within me? Put your hope in God, for I will yet praise him, my Savior and my God. **Psalm 42:6**

"Therefore, I tell you, do not worry about your life, what you will eat or drink; or about your body, what you will wear. Is not life more than food, and the body more than clothes? **Matthew 6:25 NIV**

Look at the birds of the air; they do not sow or reap or store away in barns, and yet your heavenly Father feeds them. Are you not much more valuable than they? **Matthew 6:26 NIV**

Can any one of you by worrying add a single hour to your life? **Matthew 6:27 NIV**

Therefore, do not worry about tomorrow, for tomorrow will worry about itself. Each day has enough trouble of its own. **Matthew 6:34 NIV**

I will refresh the weary and satisfy the faint." **Jeremiah 31:25 NIV**

And without faith it is impossible to please God, because anyone who comes to him must believe that he exists and that he rewards those who earnestly seek him. **Hebrews 11:6 NIV**

Cast all your anxiety on him because he cares for you. **1Peter 5:7 NIV**

The Lord is good, a refuge in times of trouble. He cares for those who trust in him. **Nahum 1:7 NIV**

For he is our God and we are the people of his pasture, the flock under his care. Today, if only you would hear his voice, **Psalm 95:7 NIV**

Are not two sparrows sold for a penny? Yet not one of them will fall to the ground outside your Father's car. **Matthew 10:29 NIV**

Wait for the Lord; be strong and take heart and wait for the Lord. **Psalm 27:14 NIV**

But if we hope for what we do not yet have, we wait for it patiently. **Romans 8:25 NIV**

But as for you, be strong and do not give up, for your work will be rewarded." **2Chronicles 15:7 NIV**

Do you see someone who speaks in haste? There is more hope for a fool than for them. **Proverb 26:20 NIV**

For it is written: "He will command his angels concerning you to guard you carefully; **Luke 4:10 NI**

Hold on to instruction, do not let it go; guard it well, for it is your life. **Proverb 4:13 NIV**

<u>*Affirmations for Worry and Anxiety:*</u>

- ❖ I will not be disturbed and worried. I put all my hopes of today and tomorrow in Christ Jesus. I sing praises to His name. Oh Lord, for you are my God, my Lord and Savior.
- ❖ I do not worry about my life. God has me covered and protected. He feeds and clothes me. I am so much more than the food and clothes He provides. I am his child and He will forever take care of me; this, I am certain.
- ❖ If birds can soar the sky without a care as to what they will eat or drink why should I? If God cares enough to sustain their lives, I know that He will sustain my life.
- ❖ I was made in God's image and was placed to rule over the creatures of the land and sea. Therefore, I know I am much more valuable than they and I am protected.
- ❖ I do not waste time worrying about things beyond my control. It does not benefit me; but instead, I give it to God and He works it out on my behalf according to his will.

- ❖ I rejoice and praise God for each day and allow him to order my steps for the matters of today. I am not burdened with matters of tomorrow.
- ❖ Just as God gives me guidance and orders my steps in the present, He too will give me guidance and order my steps in the future. I walk with God day by day and glory to glory.
- ❖ When I am weary and worn with thoughts, God refreshes my mind and renews my spirit. When I am faint, God raises me up and strengthens my body.
- ❖ I am not consumed with worry. I have complete trust that God will take control of every situation that concerns me. I have strong faith in my God because without faith it is impossible to please him.
- ❖ God cares for me and He wants the best for my life therefore; I cast all my cares on him. He wants me to have, joy, peace, happiness, love, companionship and prosperity. God wants my complete healing for every ailment and situation that I am confronted with according to his perfect will for my life.
- ❖ My God is good. When I am troubled He is a safe place. He is my refuge. He is my covering and shield. He is my protection. He is my God. My God is good.
- ❖ I do not see, yet I hope and I trust in God, as I wait patiently. My God always comes through for He is mighty and awesome.
- ❖ I do not give up. I am strong and I stand firm in the name of Jesus. I will be rewarded for my hard work and sacrifice if it be his will.

- ❖ I do not speak nor do I move haste fully out of anxiety. If I do, I am a fool. But I remain calm and still as I meditate and wait on God.
- ❖ I hold tight to the word of God and I hide it inside my heart. I guard and protect it carefully for it is my life.

Greif & Sorrow:

For his anger endureth but a moment; in his favor is life; weeping may endure for a night, but joy cometh in the morning. **Psalms 30:5 KJV**

My soul is weary with sorrow; strengthen me according to your word. **Psalm 119:28 NIV**

You then, my son, be strong in the grace that is in Christ Jesus. **2 Timothy 2:1 NIV**

In my distress I called upon the Lord, and cried unto my God: he heard my voice out of his temple, and my cry came before him, even into his ears. **Psalms 18:6 KJV**

Very truly I tell you, you will weep and morn while the world rejoices, you will grieve, but your grief will turn to joy. **John 16:20 NIV**

Indeed, he was ill, and almost died. But God had mercy on him, and not on him only but also on me to spare me sorrow upon sorrow. **Philippians 2:27 NIV**

The light shines in the darkness, and the darkness has not overcome it. **John 1:5 NIV**

3 The cords of death entangled me, the anguish of the grave came over me/ I was overcome by distress and sorrow. 4 Then I called on the name of the Lord: "Lord, save me!" **Psalms 116:3-4**

The Lord protects the unwary; when I was brought low, he saved me. **Psalms 116:6 NIV**

Return to your rest my soul, for the Lord has been good to you. **Psalms 116:7 NIV**

8 For you, Lord, have delivered me from death, my eyes from tears, my feet from stumbling, 9 that I may walk before the Lord in the land of the living. **Psalms 116:8-9 NIV**

Those who sow with tears will reap songs of joy. **Psalm 126:5 NIV**

Hear my cry, O God; listen to my prayer. **Psalm 61:1 NIV**

Praise be to the Lord, for he has heard my cry for mercy. **Psalm 28:6 NIV**

A time to weep and a time to laugh, a time to mourn and a time to dance, **Ecclesiastes 3:4 NIV**

I called upon the Lord in distress; The Lord answered me, and set me in a large place. **Psalms 118:5 KJV**

2My brethren, count it all joy when ye fall into divers temptations; 3Knowing this, that the trying of your faith worketh patience. **James 1:2-3 KJV**

He will yet fill your mouth with laughter and your lips with shouts of joy. **Job 8:21 NIV**

Light shines on the righteous and joy on the upright in heart. **Psalms 97:11 NIV**

Who shall separate us from the love of Christ? Shall tribulation, or distress, or persecution, or famine, or nakedness, or peril, or sword? **Romans 8:35 KJV**

Hear me when I call, O God of my righteousness: thou hast enlarged me when I was in distress; have mercy upon me, and hear my prayer. **Psalms 4:1 KJV**

In my distress I called upon the Lord, and cried to my God: and he did hear my voice out of his temple, and my cry did enter into his ears. **2 Samuel 22:7**

...weeping may endure for a night, but joy cometh in the morning. **Psalms 30:5 KJV**

And provide for those who grieve in Zion- to bestow on them a crown of beauty instead of ashes, the oil of joy instead of morning, and a garment of praise instead of a spirit of despair. **Isaiah 61:3 NIV**

Affirmations for Greif:

- ❖ I cry out to God from the depths of my soul and He hears my prayers. He comforts me and sooths my aching heart in the time of sorrow.

- ❖ Through all heartache and pain, God yet, shines his light upon me and plants joy in my heart because I am his child and He loves me.
- ❖ I praise God at all times because He always hears my cry and shows me mercy. He removes the pain and suffering and restores joy to my heart.
- ❖ In due time, my God will indeed fill my lips with laughter and my spirit with joy. I trust and believe in my heart that the Lord can and will do these things for me.
- ❖ No matter how much hurt, pain and distress I may experience, I will never doubt or lose faith in God. Nothing will ever separate me from His love. I will endure to the end because the Lord is my strength.
- ❖ I sing and rejoice in the name of Jesus because God covers me in his mercy; and He will remove all sorrow, pain and restore everlasting joy to my heart.
- ❖ I may weep for a season but God will restore joy to my heart. He will lift all my burdens and replace them with hope, joy and laughter. He is the healer of my soul and I am full with life and love.
- ❖ The more I meditate in the word of God, the stronger I get and the lighter my burdens become. My sorrow is lifted and my soul is renewed.
- ❖ Sorrow and sadness will not triumph over me. I am made strong by the grace of Jesus Christ. I have the power to defeat

the spirit of sorrow. I am more than a conqueror and I declare that I have a joyful spirit full of live and laughter.

- ❖ My soul remains at rest during troubling times because my God is with me. He is always good to me and He keeps my mind at peace; because I know my God will remove all burdens and heartaches from my life.
- ❖ God delivers me from death and sorrow. He dries the tears from my eyes. He picks me up and holds me steady so that I will not fall. He strengthens me and gives me new life.
- ❖ This time of sorrow is only for a season. For every tear I cry, God will return my joy ten folds in the name of Jesus.
- ❖ Darkness has no place in the kingdom of God therefore, Gods shines his light on me and removes all darkness and pain that is in my life.
- ❖ Although I experience grief, pain and heartache, I still rejoice in the Lord, for this pain allows me to grow stronger in patience, wisdom and faith for whatever I may face in the future. Through it all, God is with me and He will see me through.

Scriptures for Envy:

Love is patient, love is kind. It does not envy, it does not boast, it is not proud. **1Corinthians 13:4 NIV**

So not envy the violent or choose any of their ways. **Proverbs 3:31 NIV**

For where you have envy and selfish ambition, there you find disorder and every evil practice. **James 3:16 NIV**

Do not let your heart envy sinners, but always be zealous for the fear of the Lord. Proverbs **23:17 NIV**

A heart at peace give life to the body, but envy rots the bones. **Proverbs 14:30 NIV**

Therefore, rid yourself of all malice and all deceit, hypocrisy, envy, and slander of every kind. **1Peter 2:1 NIV**

20 Idolatry and witchcraft; hatred, discord, jealousy, fits of rage, selfish ambition, dissensions, factions 21 and envy; drunkenness, orgies and the like. I warn you as I did before, that those who live like this will not inherit the kingdom of God. **Galatians 5:20-21 NIV**

Let us not become conceited, provoking and envying each other. **Galatians 5:26 NIV**

He has so many flocks and herds and servants that the Philistines envied him. **Genesis 26:14 NIV**

For I envied the arrogant when I saw the prosperity of the wicked. **Psalm 72:3 NIV**

19"Here comes that dreamer"! they said to each other. 20" Come now, let's kill him and throw him into one of these cisterns and say that a ferocious animal devoured him. Then we'll see what comes of his dreams," **Genesis 37:19-20**

You are still worldly. For since there is jealousy and quarreling among you, are you not worldly? Are you not acting like mere humans? **1Corinthians 3:3 NIV**

Do not be overcome by evil, but overcome evil with good. **Romans 12:21 NIV**

Each one should test their own actions. Then they can take pride in themselves alone, without comparing themselves to someone else. **Galatians 6:4 NIV**

Affirmations for Envy:

- ❖ I show the love of God to others. I am patient and kind. I am not jealous of others because God provides all my needs. I am humble, and I respect my brothers and sisters. I care about their welfare and celebrate in their successes.
- ❖ I choose the ways of God and not of those who are envious. I operate in love and I am happy for others when they are prosperous. I know that if God can bless them, he can certainly bless me because he is not a respecter of persons.
- ❖ I pray for those who are selfish and envious of me. It was God who has blessed me and not myself. Their evil and selfish actions will trip them up and cause chaos and confusion to their life.
- ❖ I do not envy the possessions of sinners because it is only temporal. They have received their possessions through actions that go against the word of God. God will bless me in his own timing, therefore, I will continue to live a life that is pleasing to him and I will not grow weary.
- ❖ I have a heart of peace and love. I do not envy others. I am glad and rejoice in their blessing for God has no respect of person.

He has the power and the authority to bless all of His children according to His own timing.

- ❖ I do not wish ill will or hold deceit in my heart; nor do I backstab, slander nor envy others. I show Godly integrity and the character of Christ.
- ❖ I do not envy because I am a blessed child of the King. God supplies all my needs according to his riches in glory.
- ❖ I do not envy evil doers. My God has so many riches in heaven, I lack for nothing. All my needs are met.
- ❖ I am not distracted nor discouraged by the riches of the wicked. I trust in the everlasting God and remain steadfast in doing what is right according to God.
- ❖ I am not consumed by the words and actions of evil doers. I have victory. My foundation is planted on the Rock. I am not distracted but I remain focused on the things of God.
- ❖ I choose to follow Jesus and not the world. I avoid all jealousy, arguments and confusion because this is not of God.
- ❖ I am not overcome with evil. I walk in love, compassion and understanding and I overcome evil with good.
- ❖ I do not compare myself with others. I am confident, and I take pride in myself as a child of God by maintaining my appearance, eating healthy meals and getting the proper amount of rest and exercise needed to function at my optimum level.
- ❖ I am a unique being created by God, the Father! I love who I am. My spirit radiates with love. I am filled with the joy of Christ. My smile is as bright as the sun. My eyes are a window

to my beautiful soul. I am filled with the goodness of God because I am made in His perfect image. The love of God is all over me. I attract all that is pure and good in His sight. I leap with excitement because I have unspeakable joy in my heart that the world can never take away. Thank you, Jesus! Amen!

Unbreakable

Shannon Cromwell Brown

(Samuel, Alexia, Antonio & mother)

Unbreakable

About the Book...

Do you know how to become "Unbreakable?" I would like to introduce to you my new book, UNBREAKABLE...Defying Gravity with the Word of God!!! Have you ever just needed a word of encouragement? Something specific & especially designed for your situation? Have you ever walked through the valley of the shadow of death dealing with issues such as enemies, betrayal, failing health, finances, heartache, or simply being lost and needing guidance in life? Well, this book will definitely, bless you. It will help you to focus on God. It will help you to build your faith and remain strong during the battle. It will help you to become a fierce lion ready for the kill. In life sometimes, you may stumble, or you may fall, but with God, you can make it through. I assure you my friends, that you will not break... but in fact, you will become UNBREAKABLE!!!

About the Author...

Shannon Cromwell Brown is a native of Charleston, SC. The former pageant girl holds a B.S. in Psychology from South Carolina State University and a M.Ed. in Rehabilitation Counseling from the University of South Carolina, School of Medicine. She has worked over 20 years in counseling across the states of South Carolina, Tennessee and Mississippi in disciplines of Marriage and Family, Individual and Adolescent Counseling. As the Creator and Director of the Counseling Outreach Ministry of her local church, Shannon enjoys building the self-esteem of men, women and children through christian counseling and though various inner-city programs and projects. She enjoys the beach, traveling, physical fitness, writing and spending time with her family.

www.ingramcontent.com/pod-product-compliance
Lightning Source LLC
Chambersburg PA
CBHW071126090426
42736CB00012B/2031